IN A
HURRY
COOKBOOK

W9-CFL-975

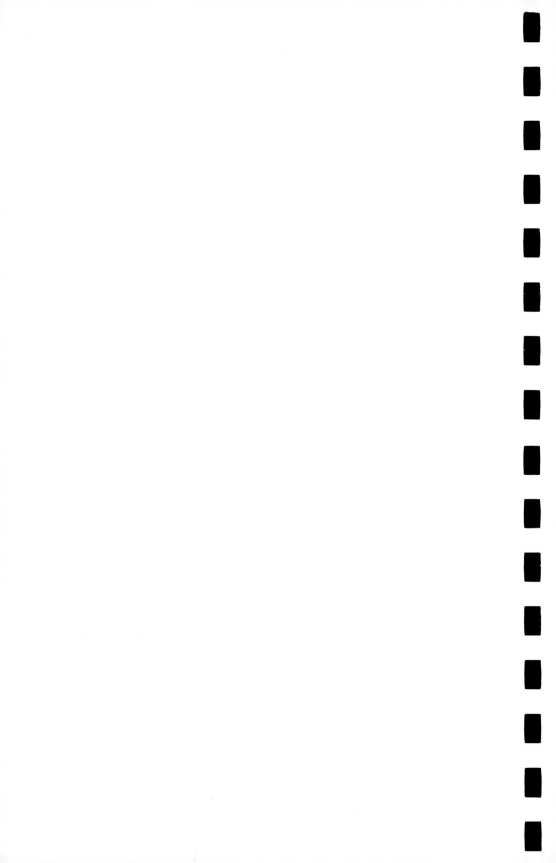

The Philadelphia Inquirer

In A Hurry Cookbook

ELAINE TAIT

THE MIDDLE ATLANTIC PRESS
Wilmington, Delaware

IN A HURRY COOKBOOK

A MIDDLE ATLANTIC PRESS BOOK

Copyright © 1988 by Philadelphia Newspapers, Inc.

All rights reserved. No part of this publication may be
reproduced or transmitted in any form or by any means,
electronic or mechanical, including photocopy, recording,
or any information storage and retrieval system, without
permission in writing from the publisher.

First Middle Atlantic Press printing, 1988

ISBN: 0-912608-60-9

The Middle Atlantic Press, Inc.
848 Church Street
Wilmington, Delaware 19899

Distributed by:
National Book Network, Inc.
4720 A Boston Way
Lanham, Maryland 20706

MANUFACTURED IN THE UNITED STATES OF AMERICA

In a Hurry

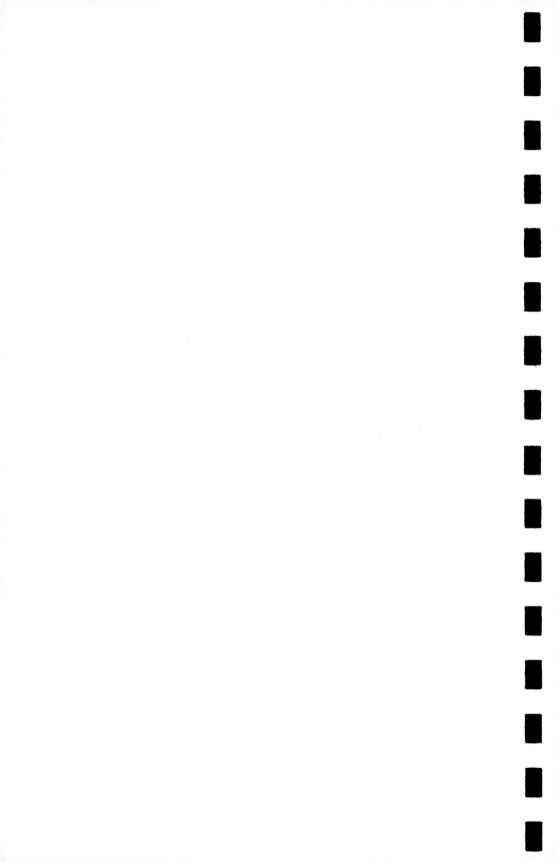

I n a Hurry was named by a newly single Inquirer editor, who admitted that he dreamed up the series hoping that it would help him to cope with the business of getting his own meals for the first time in his life.

I, his food writer, was to create menus and give recipes for meals that even a beginning cook could prepare in less than an hour. Although he didn't specify, I added my own requirement that mixes and prepared foods be kept to a minimum and fresh foods be used wherever possible.

Finding the material for the series wasn't difficult for me; it was the way I cooked on all but special occasions. But I questioned the value in putting into recipe form what I was certain most cooks already knew.

That early editor was fast and firm in assuring me that his was not a unique situation. He was convinced that the world as we knew it was crammed with cooks who drew blanks when it came time to shop for, plan and cook everyday meals. Later, when my current editor arrived on the scene and expressed the same sentiments, I, too, was convinced.

So for seven years — maybe more, I'm not good at counting — I've been cooking up In a Hurry meals for Philadelphia Inquirer readers and, more recently, for this collection.

The recipes reflect my own tastes, in that as I became more health conscious, I cooked more chicken, fish, vegetables and pasta and ate less red meat and fewer desserts. Although desserts were included with each of the original In a Hurry menus, I've come to feel that most of us don't automatically serve dessert with every meal. So I've collected my favorites from the series into a chapter that lets you be the judge of whether or not to end a meal sweetly.

All of the recipes specify conventional direct-heat cooking largely because the series was born at a time when neither I nor most of my Philadelphia-area readers were sold on the merits of microwaving. But those who use microwaves regularly will find that the recipes adapt quite easily in almost every case.

There are 75 menus — each built around a featured dish. Menus featuring poultry main dishes are collected in one chapter; those featuring meat, vegetables, seafood or pasta have their own chapters. Almost every menu includes a recipe or two for an accompaniment.

You'll find that you will be given recipes for every starred dish on the menu but not for some of the basic dishes such as rice or steamed vegetables. If you need recipes for these — and most cooks know these preparations by heart — you can find them in a good general cookbook. Many recipes are followed by related cooking tips (my equivalent of margin notes), nuggets of information I hope you'll find interesting and/or useful.

— *Elaine Tait*

•

If this book is helpful, if it makes sense and is easy to read and use, it will be because some very special people have contributed their time and considerable talents to that end. They include former Inquirer editor Don Clippinger, who had the idea for In a Hurry; food editor Ken Bookman who encouraged me to continue with the series; David Milne, who designed the book, and Helen Driggs, who assisted with production; Bob Greenberg, who spurred us all on, and, last and certainly not least, Martha Hewson, who collected the original material, refined it, classified it, saw that it was laid out properly and even, bless her, reported with unfailing enthusiasm on the In a Hurry meals she prepared for her young husband while all of this was going on.

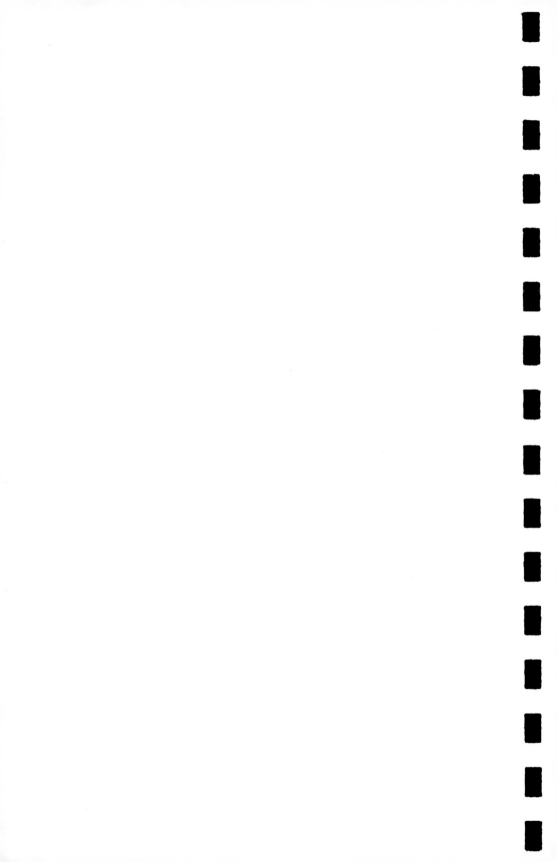

Pasta

The Philadelphia Inquirer / SARAH LEEN

Tortellini in Gorgonzola Mayonnaise is really just a fancy name for macaroni salad, but this dish is special enough to serve at a party.

Laguna Linguine

L aguna Linguine is our name for a sunny, California-style pasta dish that's ideal for cooks who want something special to serve but haven't a whole lot of time to fix it. Start with stuffed mushrooms that can be assembled with ease in the morning, then baked in a fast 15 minutes.

Offer the mushrooms with a glass of white wine while you put the water on to boil for the pasta that comes next. Like the mushrooms, the sauce for the linguine can be almost completely prepared in the morning, then finished while the pasta cooks.

A simple salad such as Belgian endive and pimento with mustard vinaigrette would round out the meal nicely.

★ Mediterranean Mushrooms

¾ pound large white mushrooms
3 to 4 tablespoons butter, divided
1 small onion, finely chopped
2 tablespoons pine nuts
1 package (10 ounces) frozen spinach, defrosted
½ cup heavy cream
½ cup freshly grated Parmesan cheese, divided
Salt and freshly ground pepper to taste

• Wipe mushrooms clean, if necessary. Remove and reserve stems. Saute the mushroom caps for a minute or two in two tablespoons of the butter. Remove and set aside.

• Chop stems finely and saute for about two minutes with the chopped onion in the same butter you used to saute the caps. Add an additional tablespoon of butter, if necessary. Stir in pine nuts.

• Remove excess water from defrosted spinach. You should have about one-half cup of spinach left. Chop spinach finely, and stir into the mushroom mixture with remaining one tablespoon butter, the cream and half the Parmesan cheese. Add salt and pepper.

• Place mushroom caps in an ovenproof baking dish. Sprinkle each cap with some of the remaining grated Parmesan cheese. Bake at 400 degrees for 15 minutes.

• Note: Mushrooms may be stuffed in advance and refrigerated until baking time.

— *Makes four appetizer servings.*

★ Laguna Linguine

3 tablespoons olive oil
3 cloves garlic
2 cans (6½ ounces each) minced clams
1 bottle (8 ounces) clam juice
½ cup dry white wine
Hot red pepper flakes to taste
1 can (14 ounces, undrained weight)
 artichoke hearts
14 oil-cured black olives, pitted
1 pound linguine, cooked and drained
1 tablespoon butter
2 tablespoons minced parsley

• Heat olive oil in a medium-size skillet. Crush two cloves of garlic with a mallet or the flat side of a knife blade. Mince remaining clove. Add crushed cloves of garlic to oil, and simmer for about two minutes. Garlic should not be allowed to brown, or it will become bitter. Remove and discard the crushed garlic and add the minced garlic to the oil in the skillet.

• Drain minced clams, and add liquid from clams to the oil and garlic, reserving clams. Add bottled clam juice, wine and red pepper flakes to taste. Cook, uncovered, about 15 minutes, over medium heat. Stir in artichoke hearts and olives, and one can of the drained clams. Simmer for five minutes.

• At serving time, toss remaining drained clams with drained and still hot linguine, butter and parsley. Divide pasta among plates. Spoon sauce over each plate. Olives, artichoke hearts and clams are salty, so additional salt should not be required.

• Note: Sauce may be made in advance.

— *Makes four to five servings.*

Confetti Fettuccine

Confetti Fettuccine won't remind you of something from your grandmother's kitchen. This is a lighter pasta designed for the good new days when even Grandma cares about eating for health.

A small amount of lean chicken breast, cut into julienne strips, makes the recipe meaty without causing cholesterol worries. Olive oil is used in modest amounts — just enough to add flavor and to keep sauteing chicken and vegetables from sticking to the pan. For salt, let your conscience be your guide. Red ripe tomatoes are seeded but not peeled for the dish. Removal of the seeds keeps the dish from being watery. Leaving the tomato skin gives the dish more valuable fiber.

To cut the chicken into julienne strips, first freeze it just until it is firm. Then slice thinly and, stacking two or three slices, cut across so that each piece is the thickness of a wooden match. Blot the defrosted chicken pieces carefully with a paper towel before stir-frying.

There is a modest amount of sauce to the dish. If you yearn for more, simply add rich chicken stock. If desired, thicken the sauce with a small amount of cornstarch dissolved in chicken broth.

Creamy Cucumber Salad makes a nice accompaniment.

★ Confetti Fettuccine

¼ cup olive oil, divided
1 large chicken breast, skinned, boned
    and cut into julienne strips
1 large onion, coarsely chopped
1 sweet red pepper and 1 sweet green pepper,
    cut into julienne strips
2 cloves garlic, minced
1 teaspoon red pepper flakes, or less
Salt to taste
2 large tomatoes, seeds removed, diced
1 pound cooked fettuccine
Freshly grated Parmesan cheese

• In large, high-sided saute pan, heat two tablespoons of the oil. Add chicken strips and saute, stirring constantly, until chicken pieces whiten,

4

in one to two minutes. Using slotted spoon, remove chicken from pan, and set aside.

• Add remaining two tablespoons of oil to pan. Heat until oil is sizzling. Add onion and peppers. Stir-fry to soften (about 10 minutes). Add chicken, garlic and pepper flakes, and season with salt. Cook two to three minutes. Add tomatoes. Heat until tomatoes are warmed through. Toss with well-drained, freshly cooked fettuccine to blend well. Serve immediately with freshly grated Parmesan.

— *Makes six servings.*

★ Creamy Cucumber Salad

> *2 medium cucumbers*
> *Salt*
> *1 small onion, peeled, sliced*
> *1 tablespoon vinegar*
> *1 teaspoon sugar*
> *½ cup plain yogurt*

• Peel and slice cucumbers. Salt and set aside in a colander to drain for 10 minutes. Mix remaining ingredients and add to drained cucumbers.

— *Makes about three cups.*

Sea Shells
With Tuna-Lemon Sauce

★ **Hot Buttered Tomato Juice**
Beans With Garlic Vinaigrette
★ **Sea Shells With Tuna-Lemon Sauce**

The refrigerator is empty and you're too tired to go shopping. Time to raid the pantry! Two shelf staples that need little else to make them into a big cold-weather main dish are shell-shaped pasta and canned tuna. Although any shape of pasta would work almost as well, there's something so pleasing about the way the shells scoop the tuna and sauce that we'd recommend them over linguine, spaghetti or fettuccine.

For a salad, reach for a can of green beans or artichoke hearts. Drain the vegetables, toss with garlic dressing and sprinkle with sesame seeds.

Need a first course? Hot Buttered Tomato Juice would take the chill off any day. The whole meal will take less than half an hour to assemble, leaving you relaxed, with the time to build a cozy fire. Or a snowman.

★ Sea Shells With Tuna-Lemon Sauce

1 pound seashell macaroni
¼ pound butter
2 cloves garlic, minced
1 teaspoon minced parsley
¼ teaspoon basil
Grated rind of ½ lemon
1 can (6½ ounces) chunk tuna, drained
Pepper to taste
2 teaspoons flour blended
with ¼ cup dry white wine
Grated Parmesan cheese

• Cook macaroni according to package directions. While macaroni cooks, melt butter in large skillet. Add garlic, parsley, basil, lemon rind and drained tuna. Cook, stirring gently, until flavors blend, about 10 minutes. Season to taste with pepper (there should be enough salt in the tuna to make more of it unnecessary).

• Stir in flour and wine mixture. Cook until sauce thickens. Drain the

6

cooked macaroni, and combine with hot sauce. Sprinkle with grated cheese and serve.

— *Makes six servings.*

★ Hot Buttered Tomato Juice

¼ cup butter
¼ cup chopped onion
2 cans (18 ounces each) tomato juice
2 cans (10½ ounces each) beef broth
Dash hot-pepper sauce
Dash Worcestershire sauce

• Melt butter, add onion, and cook until onion softens. Add juice, broth, hot-pepper sauce and Worcestershire. Heat to boiling, then serve.

— *Makes six servings.*

TIP/*TUNA*

• **Chunk tuna,** which is less expensive than solid pack, blends in nicely with the other ingredients in Sea Shells With Tuna-Lemon Sauce.

Ziti, Olive Pizza Style

The success of olives in a pizza topping prompted a search for a quickly made pasta dish with similar texture and flavor. The result is a recipe in which ziti or rigatoni is sauced with the same ingredients we loved on our pizza.

This is pretty substantial fare, and we'd like it for a weekday dinner served with spinach salad, some crusty Italian bread and a glass of lusty red wine.

★ Ziti, Olive Pizza Style

1 pound ziti or rigatoni
3 tablespoons olive oil
2 cloves garlic, finely chopped
½ pound mushrooms, sliced
1 pound canned tomatoes,
    chopped and liquid reserved
½ cup green olives, sliced
10 very thin pepperoni slices
¼ teaspoon dried oregano
Freshly ground pepper
½ pound shredded mozzarella
3 tablespoons grated Parmesan cheese
Salt to taste

• Cook ziti in boiling salted water until al dente. While ziti cooks, heat olive oil in a large pan. Add garlic and mushrooms, and saute over medium heat until mushrooms are cooked through, about five minutes. Stir in tomatoes, reserved liquid, olives and pepperoni slices. Heat through.

• Drain pasta well, and combine with tomato mixture, oregano and pepper. Add mozzarella and grated Parmesan a little at a time. Taste and add salt if necessary. Cook, over medium heat, until cheese melts. Mozzarella will be stringy.

— *Makes four servings.*

Indian Summer Pasta

If you own a food processor, you can cook up our Indian Summer Pasta from beginning to end in less than 30 minutes. If you have to chop the ingredients by hand, it will take a few minutes longer, the total time depending upon your manual dexterity. But either way, the recipe is a snap to fix and a hearty, economical dish that your family and friends should enjoy.

If you think you must have meat with the dish, serve it with grilled lamb chops that you've brushed before cooking with garlic-flavored oil.

★ Indian Summer Pasta

1 medium eggplant
1 large zucchini
1 large onion
1 medium green pepper
1 large clove garlic
3 tablespoons oil
¼ cup chopped fresh basil
1 dried red pepper, crumbled
Salt to taste
1 can (14½ ounces) stewed tomatoes
1 package (16 ounces) cut, tube-shaped
*   pasta such as penne, ziti or mostaccioli*
1 cup freshly grated Parmesan cheese

• Cut eggplant into quarters and slice in processor or by hand. Repeat with zucchini, onion, green pepper. Chop garlic finely and saute for five minutes with the cut vegetables in hot oil in a large skillet. Stir frequently. Add fresh basil, dried pepper, salt and tomatoes, and cook over high heat for 10 more minutes while cooking pasta.

• Cook pasta al dente according to package directions. Drain well and serve with hot sauce. Sprinkle with grated cheese and pass some additional grated cheese when serving.

— *Makes six servings.*

Steak and Pasta Salad

★ **White Gazpacho With Grapes**
★ **Steak and Pasta Salad**

Gazpacho, the uncooked Spanish vegetable soup once considered fashionable is now old hat. What's newer is white gazpacho, another easy to make, uncooked soup with Spanish origins. Although white gazpacho is traditionally made with ground almonds, ground sunflower seeds make a flavorful and less expensive soup.

If you're in a super hurry, use packaged croutons to garnish the soup. Otherwise, make your own by frying a slice or two of day-old bread (cubed, crusts removed) in garlic oil a minute or two then draining the croutons on a paper towel.

Cold roast beef is a familiar addition to summer menus. But for the cook who hasn't time to cook a roast and who doesn't want to pay the deli prices for already-cooked beef, we suggest cold steak, cubed and combined with curly spinach noodles, artichoke hearts, hearts of palm and red onion rings in a wonderful main dish salad. The steak cooks in just a few minutes, just long enough to sear each side well.

★ White Gazpacho With Grapes

1 cup salted sunflower seeds
2 cloves garlic, minced
¾ cup fresh bread crumbs, soaked in milk
½ cup virgin olive oil
4 cups well-chilled chicken stock,
*   fat removed*
3 tablespoons white vinegar
Salt, white pepper to taste
2 cups seedless grapes
Garlic croutons

• In processor, grind seeds to a smooth paste. Add chopped garlic. Drain crumbs and add to processer contents. Blend until smooth. Add olive oil in a steady stream. Add half of well-chilled stock and vinegar. Blend, season to taste and remove to tureen. Add remaining stock. Stir to blend well. Divide grapes among four bowls. Pour soup into bowls. Top with croutons.
— *Makes four servings.*

★ Steak and Pasta Salad

1-pound sirloin steak
1 tablespoon oil
3 cloves garlic, minced
Salt, pepper
½ pound spinach noodles
1 can (14 ounces) artichoke hearts
1 can (14 ounces) hearts of palm
1 red onion, sliced, separated into rings
1 sweet red pepper, cut in chunks
1 cup garlic salad dressing

• In large skillet in hot oil, sear steak on one side. Turn, cover with chopped garlic and sear second side. Turn in pan and remove from heat. Season with salt and pepper. When slightly cool, place steak on plate in refrigerator to cool further to facilitate slicing.

• Cook noodles al dente according to package directions. Drain artichoke hearts and cut into bite-size pieces. Drain hearts of palm and cut into one-inch segments. Drain noodles.

• Trim steak of fat and gristle. Cut steak into bite-size cubes. Toss steak with noodles, artichoke hearts, hearts of palm, onion, red pepper and dressing. Season to taste with salt and pepper. Although the salad benefits from standing, it can be served after just a few minutes' chilling.

— *Makes four to six servings.*

Pasta Buffet

Entertaining in the middle of a heat wave? Consider a pasta-salad buffet that offers a variety of pastas (all cooked and chilled) along with an even bigger assortment of toppings (cooked and raw) and a few delicious dressings.

Use your imagination in selecting the pasta shapes. Dense, dumpling-like cavatelli, fusilli (like coiled spaghetti) and Oriental cellophane noodles are the shapes we chose for testing the pasta-salad buffet concept. The first two are available in supermarkets; the third can be found in Asian food stores.

If money is no object, buy precooked lobster, shrimp, lump crab and roast beef or chicken for convenience. Otherwise, cook a chicken or two and offer canned clams (buy the tiny whole ones), mussels and tuna. Leftover roast beef, lamb or pork would also be delicious fixings. And, for one of our favorite pasta-salad additions, cook bacon until crisp enough to crumble.

Vegetables can be either raw or blanched. We blanched broccoli, carrots and snow peas but left tomatoes, celery, scallions and the like uncooked. Nice extras would include artichoke hearts, ripe olives and water chestnuts.

Offer at least three dressings. Plain mayonnaise, either homemade or a good commercial variety, will please conservative palates. If you'd like something zippier, add curry powder or horseradish to the mayonnaise. We also offered a hearty, garlic-flavored oil and vinegar dressing, and a dressing flavored with soy sauce and sesame oil.

Finally, provide some interesting garnish ingredients such as chopped nuts, chopped fresh cilantro, chives or basil. Although your guests will want to come up with their own combinations, here are some pasta partnerships that work particularly well:

Summer Garden.
• Cavatelli plus snow peas, radishes, broccoli, celery, carrots, scallions, tomatoes with mayonnaise dressing

Italian-American.
• Fusilli plus tomatoes, bacon, celery, scallions with mayonnaise dressing and fresh basil.

Gourmet Chicken.
• Fusilli with chicken, artichoke hearts, ripe olives, celery, scallions and broccoli with mayonnaise or Hearty Garlic Dressing.

Oriental Noodle.
• Cellophane noodles with snow peas, celery, broccoli, water chestnuts and cilantro with Oriental Dressing.

Sea Special.
• Any pasta, shellfish (lobster, crab, clam, mussels) or tuna with broccoli, snow peas, scallions, celery and mayonnaise.

Oriental Chicken.
• Cellophane noodle with chicken, broccoli, water chestnuts, scallions, cilantro and Oriental Dressing.

Antipasto.
• Cavatelli with broccoli, scallions, olives, artichoke hearts, radishes, tuna and Hearty Garlic Dressing.

★ Oriental Dressing

½ cup soy sauce

6 tablespoons vinegar

3 tablespoons sesame oil

2 cloves garlic, minced

2 teaspoons minced ginger

½ teaspoon Szechwan peppercorn powder

• Combine ingredients. Let stand to improve flavors.
— *Makes about one cup.*

★ Hearty Garlic Dressing

⅔ cup olive oil or salad oil

¼ cup wine vinegar

2 cloves garlic, crushed

2 teaspoons salt

⅛ teaspoon pepper

½ teaspoon dried tarragon,
    or 1½ teaspoons fresh, chopped

• In a jar, blend ingredients thoroughly. Cover and set aside several hours to blend flavors.
— *Makes about one cup.*

TIP/*PASTA*

• **Cellophane noodles** do not require cooking. Simply soak in hot water until noodles soften (about 30 minutes), drain and coat lightly with salad oil. Cook other pasta al dente, according to package directions. Drain, cool and coat lightly with salad oil.

Penne With Grated Zucchini and Parmesan

Spinach and Red Onion Rings
★ **Honey-Mustard Vinaigrette**
Cold Shrimp
★ **Salsa Cruda**
★ **Penne With Grated Zucchini**
  and Parmesan

In Italy, there are guidelines as to which sauce belongs with which pasta shape, but American cooks have no such inhibiting rules. Penne, the quill-shape pasta, cooks to a pleasing, chewy texture that seems to call for the soft contrast of the garlic-scented zucchini and the melted cheese.

One caution is in order. The zucchini needs to drain after it is grated. Otherwise it will make the sauce much too watery. Use firm, small-to-medium-size zucchini for best results.

For a nice warm-weather meal, begin with cold shrimp served with Salsa Cruda and offer a salad of spinach and red onion rings tossed with Honey-Mustard Vinaigrette.

★ Penne With Grated Zucchini and Parmesan

1 pound medium zucchini
1 pound penne
2 tablespoons butter
1 tablespoon olive oil
1 large clove garlic, minced
¼ teaspoon red pepper flakes or to taste
⅔ cup freshly grated Parmesan cheese
Additional Parmesan for the table

• Grate the zucchini. Place in colander, and let drain for about 15 minutes to release excess moisture.

• Cook penne in boiling salted water according to package directions. When penne is almost cooked, press zucchini against colander to remove remaining moisture.

• Heat butter and oil together in large skillet until mixture begins to bubble. Add grated zucchini, and cook about three minutes — no more. Add garlic, and cook one more minute, stirring constantly. Stir in pepper flakes and the ⅔ cup of grated Parmesan. Heat one minute more. Toss with well-drained penne. Pass additional cheese at the table. (Additional salt should not be needed because the cheese is salty.)

— *Makes four servings.*

★ Salsa Cruda

2 large tomatoes
2 pickled jalapeno peppers
10 sprigs fresh coriander
1 small clove garlic
½ teaspoon salt

• Cut tomatoes and peppers coarsely. Remove stems from coriander and chop leaves finely. Chop garlic finely. Mix ingredients, stirring well to blend flavors. Flavor improves on standing but sauce can be used immediately.

— *Makes about one cup.*

★ Honey-Mustard Vinaigrette

½ cup virgin olive oil
2 tablespoons wine vinegar
1 teaspoon honey
Salt, pepper to taste
Dash cayenne pepper

• Blend ingredients. Use over spinach salad.
— *Makes enough for several salads.*

Pepper Potpourri Pasta

Cherry Tomato Salad
★ **Pepper Potpourri Pasta**
Roast Chicken

For a brief time, when they are locally abundant, you can buy bright yellow, red and occasionally even rare black-skinned peppers for a fraction of their midwinter prices. 'Tis the time, then, to revel in their beauty and flavor.

Pepper Potpourri Pasta lets you mix and match pepper colors and heats to suit yourself. The dish is almost a meal in itself, with bacon and grated cheese adding to the hefty combination of green fettuccine and sauteed peppers.

While diners savor the pasta course, put the meat course — fried or roasted chicken that you've bought precooked — in the oven to heat. At serving time, grate some fresh lemon rind over the top and notice the flavor lift it gives.

Make the easiest-ever salad by drizzling cherry tomatoes with good olive oil, then sprinkling with coarse salt and a scattering of fresh basil leaves.

★ Pepper Potpourri Pasta

4 cups peppers, seeded and sliced
3 tablespoons olive oil
8 slices bacon
1 pound spinach fettuccine
½ cup freshly grated Parmesan cheese
Salt and pepper to taste

• Choose a variety of peppers, including hot peppers if desired. Saute in the olive oil until softened but still shapely.

• While the peppers cook, microwave or fry the bacon until crisp. Discard the bacon fat. Set the bacon aside.

• Cook the spinach fettuccine in boiling water according to package directions until al dente. Drain the fettuccine and toss with the sauteed peppers. Crumble the bacon and add along with the grated Parmesan cheese, salt and pepper.

— *Makes six servings.*

Pasta Salad Puttanesca

Vichyssoise
★ **Pasta Salad Puttanesca**
Grilled Chicken

Pasta Puttanesca is the popular Italian dish named for the ladies of the evening *(puttane)* who are said to have designed this quick and inexpensive dish with their own lusty appetites and demanding schedules in mind. In its original form, Pasta Puttanesca would be served warm, but for easy summer entertaining, we like a cool new form designed to be served at room temperature.

The dish is big enough to stand on its own at lunch, but it's also a nice accompaniment to a simple patio meal of grilled chicken or hamburgers. To fill out the meal, begin with a cup of well-chilled vichyssoise.

★ Pasta Salad Puttanesca

1 pound shell-shaped pasta
¾ cup olive oil
¼ cup white wine vinegar
1 teaspoon dried oregano
⅛ teaspoon dried red pepper flakes
3 cloves garlic, minced
1 cup Nicoise or California black olives
¼ cup capers, drained
6 anchovy filets, coarsely chopped
½ cup chopped Italian parsley
10 cherry tomatoes, halved
Salt to taste

● Cook pasta al dente according to package directions. Blend olive oil, wine vinegar, oregano, dried pepper flakes, garlic, olives, capers and anchovy filets.

● When pasta is cooked, drain well and let cool slightly. Pour olive oil mixture over the warm pasta and let stand while flavors blend. At last minute, toss with parsley and cherry tomatoes, and add salt to taste.

— *Makes four main-course or eight salad servings.*

Tortellini
in Gorgonzola Mayonnaise

★ **Tortellini in Gorgonzola Mayonnaise**
Grilled Steak
Stir-fry Vegetables

When you get right down to it, Tortellini in Gorgonzola Mayonnaise is just another name for macaroni salad. But thanks to the use of these small, interesting filled pastas, the salad becomes special enough to serve at a buffet party.

Tortellini are time-consuming to make at home. The dough must be mixed and rolled very thin, then cut, filled and shaped into little letter o's. But cooks in a hurry have been discovering recently that ready-made (and often excellent) tortellini are available in better food shops. Although some stores will have them available fresh, most offer frozen or dried tortellini. The latter, imported from Italy, need no refrigeration, despite their fillings.

Gorgonzola cheese blended with mayonnaise and sour cream is the final dressing, but before you add it, and while the pasta is still warm from cooking, it is mixed well with a lighter olive oil and lemon dressing and with the red onion rings and sweet red pepper that give it such happy color.

We like the pasta as a first course to be followed by a simple but substantial entree such as grilled steak with stir-fried vegetables.

★ Tortellini in Gorgonzola Mayonnaise

1 pound fresh or frozen cheese-filled
*   tortellini or one package dried*
¼ cup olive oil
Juice of ½ fresh lemon
½ red onion, sliced in rings
½ cup chopped sweet red pepper
¼ pound Gorgonzola cheese
Salt, pepper
½ cup homemade mayonnaise
¼ cup sour cream
Parsley garnish (optional)

• Cook tortellini al dente. Combine olive oil, lemon juice, onion and sweet pepper. Drain tortellini and, while still warm, toss with the oil-pepper mixture and half the cheese, crumbled. Allow to cool. Season with salt and pepper to taste.

● Mash remaining cheese and combine with mayonnaise and sour cream. Toss with tortellini. Serve immediately or allow to stand, under refrigeration, to blend flavors further. Garnish with fresh Italian parsley, if desired.

— *Makes four servings.*

TIPS/*STEAK AND MORE*

● **Steak** to be grilled should be well-trimmed. Melting fat creates a sooty, unpleasant-tasting coating on the meat. Less expensive steaks become more tender when marinated for a few hours. Ordinary vinaigrette makes an acceptable marinade.

● The name **tortellini** means small twist. In Bologna, where they originated, the filled pastas are said to resemble the navel of Venus.

● **Gorgonzola** is a mild and delicate blue-veined cheese from Italy.

● When **stir-frying** a combination of several vegetables, start with those that take longest to cook. Add one vegetable at a time, ending with those that cook quickest. Don't overcook. Stir-fry vegetables should be crisp-tender. Add seasonings such as fresh herbs near the end of cooking or their flavor will fade.

● **Sweet onions** currently popular for salads include Maui, Walla Walla or Vidalia onions. Red onions are sweet and colorful — and more widely available.

Skinny Dinners

★ **Fennel Salad Chinoise**
★ **Chinese Spaghetti or**
★ **Skinny Spaghetti**
★ **Green Beans With Sesame Oil**

A homemade Skinny Dinner is as convenient to get to the table as the commercial frozen diet entrees, but considerably less expensive. Since you are the cook, you control the ingredients. You also control the seasonings, portion size, calorie content and cooking method.

Make your Skinny Dinners exciting by relying on robust seasonings. Garlic is great. Soy sauce (use the low-sodium kind) works wonders, too. Sliced fresh ginger and curry powder are other pepper-uppers.

Stick to dishes with lots of thick flavorful sauce. Spaghetti is a diet delight when there's more sauce than spaghetti and when the sauce is made with a small amount of lean ground beef and a lot of chunky vegetables.

Reheating time will depend on the cooking method you choose — just a few minutes in the microwave, perhaps as long as a half-hour in the oven.

For a low-calorie, East-meets-West meal, serve either of these spaghetti dishes with Green Beans With Sesame Oil and a salad dressed with rice wine vinegar and sugar.

★ Chinese Spaghetti

4 ounces lean ground beef
1 slice ginger, peeled and minced
1 clove garlic, minced
1 cup green pepper strips
1 small carrot, thinly sliced
½ cup sliced onion
1 teaspoon fermented black beans
2 tablespoons low-sodium soy sauce
1 tablespoon sherry
½ teaspoon sugar
1 cup chicken broth, divided
1 tablespoon cornstarch
6 ounces spaghetti, cooked

• In a large skillet, brown beef with ginger and garlic. Pour off excess fat. Stir-fry green pepper, carrot and onion with beef until peppers begin to soften. Stir in black beans, soy sauce, sherry, sugar and three-quarters of the chicken broth. Cook, stirring occasionally, until carrots are crisp-tender. Stir cornstarch into remaining chicken broth to dissolve. Add cornstarch mixture to pan and cook, stirring, until sauce thickens. Divide sauce into four portions. Package portions separately and freeze.

• Divide cooked spaghetti into four portions. Package each portion separately and freeze. At serving time, heat a package each of sauce and pasta. Cook in microwave or oven until defrosted and heated through. Spoon sauce over pasta and serve.

— *Makes four servings.*

★ Skinny Spaghetti

6 ounces lean ground beef
1 clove garlic, minced
1 small onion, chopped
1 small sweet red pepper, sliced
1 small green pepper, sliced
¼ cup each chopped fresh basil and parsley
1 can (1 pound) whole peeled tomatoes
Salt and pepper to taste
6 ounces spaghetti, cooked

• In nonstick skillet, brown beef with garlic, stirring to break up chunks of meat. Drain any excess fat and discard. Stir in sweet red and green pepper, and continue cooking until pepper begins to soften. Add basil, parsley and tomatoes. Season to taste with salt and pepper. Continue cooking until sauce flavors blend, about 25 minutes.

• Divide sauce into four equal portions, package separately and freeze. Divide spaghetti into four equal portions, package separately and freeze. To serve, heat one package each of sauce and spaghetti. Cook until defrosted and heated through. Serve one package of spaghetti and sauce per serving.

— *Makes four servings.*

★ Green Beans With Sesame Oil

1 pound green beans
Salt, pepper to taste
Sesame oil

• Remove stems and strings from beans. Steam or cook in boiling water until crisp-tender and still bright in color. Drain well. Season with salt, pepper and a few drops of sesame oil. Serve immediately or serve later at room temperature.

— *Makes four servings.*

★ Fennel Salad Chinoise

2 cups fresh fennel slices
2 tablespoons sugar
2 tablespoons rice wine vinegar
Salt, pepper to taste
1 tablespoon chopped fennel fronds

• Toss fennel slices with dressing made of sugar dissolved in vinegar. Season to taste with salt and pepper. Sprinkle with chopped fennel fronds.

— *Makes four servings.*

Poultry

The Philadelphia Inquirer / MYRNA LUDWIG

Take advantage of the good pan juices from Chicken With Black Beans and Garlic. Serve the dish with rice so you won't waste a drop.

Spring Tonic Soup

★ **Spring Tonic Soup**
★ **Curried Chicken Salad**

S pring Tonic Soup is what happens to chicken soup when it gets into the spirit of the season. Made with as many spring greens and herbs as you can collect, the soup is lighter than most vegetable soups.

Basic greens for this Spring Tonic Soup might include spinach, scallions, leeks, watercress and Boston lettuce. If you can find them, add lamb's-lettuce, beet greens or escarole. For the herbs, chives or Italian parsley would do for starters. If they were available, we would add a sprig or two of fresh tarragon and thyme, and a few basil leaves.

If you'd like a slightly more substantial soup, add leftover cooked rice. For a nice finishing touch, sprinkle good grated Parmesan cheese over the top at serving time.

If you want really good chicken broth for the soup, you'll make it yourself. And if you do, you'll have chicken for chicken salad, which makes a perfect luncheon follow-up for the soup.

★ Spring Tonic Soup

½ cup sliced leeks (white part only)
1 tablespoon butter
2 tablespoons oil
4 cups chicken stock, preferably homemade
1 cup shredded spinach leaves
1 cup chopped mixed raw greens
Bouquet garni (Italian parsley, chives, tarragon, thyme and basil leaves wrapped in cheesecloth)
Salt, pepper
Grated Parmesan cheese

• In large pot, saute leeks gently in butter and oil until soft, about five minutes. Add chicken stock and bring to boil. Add spinach leaves, mixed greens and bouquet garni. Cook 20 minutes, or until flavors are blended. Remove and discard bouquet garni. Season to taste with salt and pepper. Serve soup sprinkled with grated Parmesan.

— Makes four to six servings.

★ Curried Chicken Salad

1 boiled chicken used in making stock
⅔ cup good-quality mayonnaise
1 teaspoon curry powder
Salt, pepper to taste
¼ cup golden raisins
½ cup choppped celery
½ cup chopped toasted walnuts
Lettuce leaves

• Allow chicken to cool in stock. When cool, remove and discard skin and bones. Chop larger pieces into bite-size. Blend mayonnaise with curry powder and chicken. Season to taste with salt and pepper. Add raisins, celery and walnuts, blending well. Place each serving in lettuce leaves.
— *Makes four servings.*

TIPS/*CHICKEN SOUP*

• In some countries, chicken soup is thickened with **egg yolk**. A Turkish version of this soup has an enrichment of cream. Greek chicken soup, called avgolemono, is thickened with egg and has the added zest of lemon juice.

• Italian cooks beat **egg white** into a chicken soup. The appearance of the cooked egg prompted some long-ago Italian to give the soup the name stracciatella, which translates to rags and tatters. A remarkably similar Chinese soup has the whole egg beaten into the hot soup and is called egg drop or egg flower.

• The very rich **chicken stock** that serves as a base for many Chinese soups is sometimes made with pork as well as chicken.

• In a hurry to **skim the fat** from chicken stock? An ice cube floated in the soup will help to congeal the fat and make it easier to remove.

Basic Chicken Salad

In the recipe that follows, we'll show how to turn a basic chicken salad into a party salad, and then into another salad with California overtones. You'll see how easy it is to transform the same basic recipe into a delicious roast beef and potato salad with horseradish dressing, or a ham salad with raisins and nuts. And finally, again using the basic recipe as your guide, you'll be making shrimp and salmon salads.

A second basic salad, this one made with noodles and an Oriental dressing, is almost as versatile. We'll tell how to concoct a few variations.

Any of the salads would make a delicious summer meal accompanied by a super-simple salad of cold cooked vegetables with a creamy, nicely spiced dressing. We suggest green beans — lightly cooked, then chilled — topped with thick buttermilk dressing, but you could also use artichoke hearts, cooked carrots, zucchini, or a dozen other vegetables.

★ Basic Chicken Salad

3 cups cooked, boneless chicken cubes
½ cup each mayonnaise and yogurt
½ cup celery slices
½ cup chopped onion
3 tablespoons chopped parsley
Salt, pepper

• Toss chicken with mayonnaise, yogurt, celery, onion, parsley, and salt and pepper to taste until ingredients are blended well.
— *Makes four to six servings.*

Party Chicken Salad.
• For dressing, use one-half cup mayonnaise blended with one-half cup sour cream, seasoned with one teaspoon curry powder (or curry powder to taste). Add chicken and celery slices. Substitute scallions for onion. Add one-half cup chopped ripe olives and one-half cup toasted pecan halves. Season to taste with salt and pepper. Toss gently and serve.

California Chicken Salad.
• Add one tablespoon anchovy paste and one teaspoon freshly chopped tarragon to mayonnaise and yogurt. Toss chicken cubes with celery, onion, parsley, one-quarter cup toasted slivered almonds and one avocado, peeled and cubed. Season to taste. Garnish with alfalfa sprouts.

Roast Beef and Potato Salad.
• Use three cups cooked lean roast beef cubes instead of chicken. Add one tablespoon drained horseradish to mayonnaise and yogurt. Toss with celery, onion, parsley and one cup firm cooked potato cubes. (If desired, add more dressing to make salad moist.) Season with salt and pepper.

Party Ham Salad.

• Substitute three cups cooked, boneless ham cubes for chicken. Add one teaspoon salad-type mustard to mayonnaise and yogurt. Add celery, onion, parsley and one-half cup each toasted pecans and plump raisins. Season to taste. Garnish with one-quarter cup toasted coconut.

Shrimp Salad.

• Substitute three cups cooked, chopped shrimp for chicken. Add remaining ingredients, plus one cup chopped watercress and one-half cup chopped green pepper. Season to taste with salt and pepper. Garnish with cherry tomato halves and green pepper rings.

Salmon Salad.

• Substitute one one-pound can of salmon for chicken. Drain salmon, break into large pieces and toss very gently (you don't want to crush the salmon) with remaining ingredients plus two cups cooked shell macaroni, and mayonnaise and yogurt dressing to which you've added one tablespoon chopped fresh dill, one teaspoon chopped chives and one tablespoon fresh lemon juice. (If desired, add additional dressing to moisten salad.) Season with salt and pepper. Garnish with chopped carrot and more dill sprigs.

★ Basic Oriental Noodle Salad

4 cups cooked pasta
2 tablespoons each soy sauce, rice vinegar
* and sesame oil*
1 tablespoon sugar
Salt, red pepper flakes
1 cup crisp-cooked vegetables
½ cup chopped scallions

• For pasta, use Italian spiral or shell macaroni, Japanese buckwheat or Chinese noodles, cooked al dente, drained and cooled. Make dressing from soy sauce, rice vinegar, sesame oil and sugar. Taste and add salt and red pepper flakes as desired. Toss with cooked vegetables and scallions. For cooked vegetables, use broccoli florets, snow peas (cut in sections), stir-fried mushroom slices or zucchini.

• Garnish as desired with your choice of chopped fresh coriander, toasted sesame seeds, water chestnut slices or a mixture of finely shredded fresh ginger and scallions.

— *Makes four to six servings.*

Peppered Chicken

★ **Tomato-Olive Salad**
★ **Peppered Chicken**
   Rice
★ **Mediterranean Garden Medley**

Chicken, peppercorns, salt, butter and scallions are all you'll need for Peppered Chicken. The peppercorns are first pounded between sheets of paper towels to crack them and release their flavor. Next, the cracked pepper is added to melted butter and allowed to simmer a few minutes to release the pepper flavor into the butter.

Easy accompaniments might be fluffy cooked rice and a Mediterranean vegetable medley that combines eggplant, red and green pepper, onion, garlic and zucchini. Saute the eggplant in a nonstick skillet or pan sprayed with nonstick coating, and you won't add to the calories of the dish. When the eggplant chunks have browned, add the other ingredients and some oil and stir-fry until the vegetables begin to soften somewhat.

An easy salad that's in keeping with the mood of the meal is a combination of black olives and cherry tomato halves.

★ Peppered Chicken

1 teaspoon black peppercorns
3 tablespoons melted butter
2 large chicken breasts, skinned, boned
   and cut in half
4 scallions, chopped
Salt to taste

• Crush peppercorns between two heavy paper towels using a mallet or the bottom of a heavy skillet. Combine melted butter and peppercorns and cook, over low heat, for about five minutes or until flavors blend.

• Strain pepper butter through a sieve into a skillet just large enough to hold chicken breasts without crowding. When butter begins to sizzle, add chicken breasts and brown each piece on both sides. When chicken pieces are browned, add chopped scallions and reduce heat. Continue to cook until chicken is cooked through, about five to 10 minutes, depending on thickness of chicken. Salt to taste and serve, spooning any butter in pan over chicken.

— *Makes four servings.*

★ Mediterranean Garden Medley

1 small eggplant, cut in small chunks
2 tablespoons virgin olive oil
1 small onion, sliced
1 clove garlic, minced
1 medium zucchini, sliced
1 sweet red pepper, cut in strips
1 green pepper, cut in squares
Salt, pepper

• Using nonstick skillet or pan sprayed with nonstick oil coating, brown eggplant chunks on all sides. Add remaining ingredients to pan, and cook, stirring constantly, until vegetables begin to soften.

— *Makes four servings.*

★ Tomato-Olive Salad

1 pint cherry tomatoes
Juice of ½ lemon
½ teaspoon sugar
4 large basil leaves, shredded
1 tablespoon virgin olive oil
½ cup small black olives
Salt, pepper

• Cut tomatoes in half. Toss gently with lemon juice, sugar, basil leaves, olive oil, olives, salt and pepper.

— *Makes four servings.*

Chicken With Black Beans and Garlic

There is no American counterpart for the fermented black beans used in Chicken With Black Beans and Garlic. But the inexpensive, very salty little beans used as a flavoring in so many Chinese dishes are easy to find in Asian food markets. What's more, a package of the beans, once opened, can be stored nicely for months without refrigeration if kept in an airtight container.

The recipe is almost embarrassingly simple and quick to fix. To save time, boneless chicken breasts, cut into half-inch wide strips, are used.The chicken cooks with the garlic and beans through stir-frying in hot oil

Because you'll want to take advantage of the good pan juices, serve the chicken over steamed white rice with lemon-buttered fresh asparagus as the vegetable. The menu could use a bit of color, so offer orange slices and endive leaves tossed with toasted walnut pieces and a good vinaigrette for the salad.

★ Chicken With Black Beans and Garlic

1 pound boneless chicken breasts
2 tablespoons salad oil
3 cloves garlic, finely minced
3 tablespoons Chinese black beans
1 tablespoon soy sauce
1 teaspoon sugar
1 tablespoon sherry

• Cut chicken into strips about one-half-inch wide. Heat oil in a large skillet or wok. Saute chicken with garlic and black beans until chicken becomes firm and looks white. Immediately add soy sauce mixed with sugar and sherry. Stir to blend sauce with chicken pieces. Cook a minute or two longer, and serve over fluffy hot rice.
— *Makes four servings.*

★ Orange, Endive and Walnut Salad

2 large seedless oranges
1 head Belgian endive
¼ cup walnut pieces
1 tablespoon butter
Salt, pepper to taste
Vinaigrette Dressing (see recipe)

• Peel oranges, removing as much of the white membrane as possible to avoid bitterness. Slice oranges across. Arrange slices on platter. Slice endive into thin slivers; sprinkle over orange slices. Top with walnut pieces that have been sauteed in butter until slightly browned. Sprinkle lightly with salt and pepper and drizzle vinaigrette over salad at serving time.

— *Makes four servings.*

★ Vinaigrette Dressing

¼ cup good olive oil
1 tablespoon wine vinegar
½ teaspoon Dijon mustard
Pinch dried herbs
Salt and pepper to taste

• Blend ingredients well. Use as directed above.

— *Makes four servings.*

Chicken-Scallion Rolls

Avocados Stuffed With Crab
★ Chicken-Scallion Rolls
★ Mushroom Risotto
Tiny Peas

C hicken-Scallion Rolls are attractive enough to serve to your favorite guests. Once the chicken breasts are boned and pounded to an even thickness, they are spread with your choice of butters. We tested scallion, garlic, sage and basil butters, and a combination of basil, garlic, Parmesan cheese and butter, and all were delicious.

Tie the rolls with a long scallion top. You'll be surprised to find that the roll stays securely tied with this edible string.

Serve the chicken with Mushroom Risotto made with the imported short-grained rice used in Italy for this purpose. While it's more expensive than most other rice (an exception being our own wild rice, which is actually a grass seed), it makes a deliciously different starch course, well worth the extra cost. Dried mushrooms give the risotto a delicious woodsy flavor.

Tiny peas make a pleasant accompaniment.

If you feel the meal needs a first course, consider avocado shells, heaped with crabmeat and served with tarragon mayonnaise.

★ Chicken-Scallion Rolls

3 large chicken breasts, split, boned
*   and skin removed*
7 tablespoons softened butter, divided
Choice of seasonings (see directions)
Salt, pepper
6 green scallion tops
2 tablespoons oil
½ cup dry white wine

• Place each half of chicken breast between two sheets of waxed paper and pound to even thickness, using a mallet or heavy rolling pin. Trim edges to make a rectangular shape.

• Make seasoned butter by blending five tablespoons softened butter with one of the following seasonings: ½ teaspoon powdered sage, 1 clove finely minced garlic, 1 tablespoon chopped fresh basil, 2 tablespoons finely chopped scallions, or a combination of 2 tablespoons Parmesan cheese, 1 clove finely chopped garlic and 1 teaspoon chopped fresh basil.

32

• Divide seasoned butter among the six pieces of chicken, spreading each piece to about ½ inch from the edges. Season lightly with salt and pepper. Roll each piece in jelly-roll fashion, tucking in ends first.

• Soften scallion tops slightly by dipping in boiling water or placing in a microwave for a few seconds. Tie each chicken bundle loosely with one scallion top.

• Melt remaining two tablespoons butter with oil in a skillet large enough to hold all six chicken rolls without crowding. When butter begins to sizzle, add chicken rolls and cook, turning frequently, to brown all sides.

• Cover, reduce heat and cook for 10 minutes or until chicken rolls are cooked through. Remove cover, add wine and stir to dissolve browned particles in pan. Cook until wine is reduced to half its volume. Serve chicken rolls with wine and butter mixture from pan.

— *Makes six servings.*

★ Mushroom Risotto

3 dried mushrooms
3 tablespoons butter
1 onion, minced
1½ cups Italian short-grain rice
½ cup dry white wine
8 cups hot chicken broth
Salt, white pepper
½ cup grated Parmesan cheese

• Soak the mushrooms for a half-hour in ¼ cup hot water. Then drain the mushrooms, reserving the soaking water, and chop coarsely. In heavy saucepan, melt butter. Add mushrooms and onion to butter. Cook until onion is tender. Add rice, stirring to coat rice well with butter.

• Add the water in which the mushrooms have soaked, and the wine. Cook, uncovered, until liquid is absorbed. Add hot chicken broth, a cup at a time, cooking until each addition of broth is absorbed by the rice. When all the broth has been absorbed (about 20 minutes), taste and add salt and pepper as needed. At serving time, stir in grated cheese.

— *Makes six servings.*

Curry-Sauteed Chicken
With Sweet and Hot Apricots

★ **Curry-Sauteed Chicken**
  With Sweet and Hot Apricots
★ **Confetti Corn and Potatoes**

Consider fresh apricots as the starting point for a sweet and hot condiment that's just right with curried chicken breasts. The golden fruits shed their stones easily and don't require peeling. Simply slice, saute in some butter and orange marmalade, and season with lemon and hot-pepper flakes. The sauce is table-ready in minutes.

Farm-fresh corn requires somewhat more handling, but here, too, the work is fast and easy. Husk the corn, remove kernels from the cob with a sharp knife, and saute with diced cooked potatoes, minced sweet pepper, and onion for a great in-season accompaniment to the chicken and apricots. The small, waxy new potatoes suitable for the dish can be pared more easily after they have been cooked, but they can be left unpeeled.

★ Curry-Sauteed Chicken
With Sweet and Hot Apricots

2 tablespoons salad oil
3 large cloves garlic, minced
2 boneless, skinless chicken breasts, halved
4 tablespoons butter, divided
10 apricots, pitted and sliced
¼ cup orange marmalade
1 teaspoon lemon juice
½ teaspoon red pepper flakes
Curry powder to taste
½ cup finely chopped onion
Salt and pepper to taste

• Pour the oil and sprinkle the garlic over chicken breasts in a shallow dish. Set aside to marinate while preparing apricots.

• Heat two tablespoons of the butter, and saute the apricots in the hot butter until the fruit begins to soften. Stir in marmalade, lemon juice and pepper flakes. Cook over low heat for five minutes. Keep warm.

34

• Wipe garlic and excess oil from the chicken. (A small amount of oil should remain on the breasts and will be useful in preventing the chicken from sticking during cooking.)

• Heat a saute pan without oil. Place chicken breasts in the hot pan, and sear on both sides. (A spatula will help to keep the meat from sticking to the pan.) If necessary, a small amount of oil from the marinade may be added to the pan.

• Sprinkle chicken with curry powder as it browns. Add onion and remaining two tablespoons of butter to the pan. Reduce heat, and cook over low heat until chicken is cooked through, about five minutes, more if the chicken pieces are thick. Season with salt and pepper. Serve each portion with a side serving of apricots.

— *Makes four servings.*

★ Confetti Corn and Potatoes

2 large ears white or yellow corn
4 small waxy new potatoes, cooked
2 tablespoons oil
1 small onion, finely chopped
½ sweet red pepper, diced
¼ teaspoon cumin
1 tablespoon butter
Salt and pepper to taste

• Remove husks and silk from corn, and slice kernels from the cobs with a sharp slicing knife. Pare cooked potatoes and cut into large cubes. Heat a large saute pan. Add the oil, and when it sizzles, add potatoes with onion and sweet pepper.

• Saute, stirring frequently, until potatoes begin to color. Stir in corn, cumin and butter. Season with salt and pepper. Cook, stirring, until corn cooks, about a minute or two, and the flavors blend.

— *Makes four servings.*

Broccoli-Chicken Salad

> ★ **Artichoke Frittata**
> ★ **Broccoli-Chicken Salad**
> ★ **Ginger Dressing**
> ★ **Couscous Salad**

H ere is a picnic plan ready to set into motion at the first balmy day. Marinated artichoke hearts give flavor and substance to the Italian appetizer omelet known as frittata. Broccoli-Chicken Salad can be used to fill pita sandwiches at home or at the picnic site.

Couscous Salad, perfect for a picnic because it needs no refrigeration, starts with the new, convenient form of that grain available in many supermarkets.

★ Artichoke Frittata

> *1 jar (6½ ounces) marinated artichokes*
> *6 eggs*
> *Salt and pepper to taste*
> *¼ cup freshly grated Parmesan cheese*

• Remove artichokes from jar, reserving the marinade. Chop artichokes coarsely, and saute in two tablespoons of the reserved marinade in an ovenproof nine-inch skillet for one minute.

• Beat eggs to blend. Season lightly with salt and pepper. Pour egg mixture over the artichokes and cook over medium heat until eggs have set in an even layer, about two to three minutes.

• Sprinkle surface with grated cheese, and place skillet under preheated broiler for a minute or two to brown and cook the frittata surface. Serve at room temperature, cut into wedges.

— *Makes four servings.*

★ Broccoli-Chicken Salad

> *1 roaster chicken breast, cooked*
> *2 cups cooked broccoli florets*
> *1 small red onion, chopped*
> *Ginger Dressing (see recipe)*
> *Salt and pepper to taste*
> *4 small pita bread pockets*

• Remove skin and bone from chicken breast, and cut meat into large cubes. Toss with broccoli, onion and Ginger Dressing. Season to taste with salt and pepper. Serve stuffed into small pita bread pockets.

— *Makes four servings.*

★ Ginger Dressing

2 tablespoons fresh ginger, peeled
and coarsely chopped
2 tablespoons Dijon mustard
2 teaspoons hoisin sauce
1 tablespoon balsamic vinegar
1 tablespoon light soy sauce
Cayenne pepper to taste
1 tablespoon sherry
2 tablespoons sesame oil
¼ cup salad oil

• Blend ingredients in blender or processor. Use as directed above.

— *Makes about 1½ cups.*

★ Couscous Salad

1 cup couscous
1½ cups chicken stock
1 cup coarsely chopped cucumber
6 scallions, coarsely chopped
¼ cup raisins
¼ cup chopped fresh parsley
⅛ teaspoon hot red pepper flakes
1 teaspoon dried mint
½ teaspoon ground cumin
6 tablespoons extra-virgin olive oil
Juice of 1 large lemon
Salt and pepper to taste

• Prepare couscous according to package directions with the chicken stock. Toss warm couscous with cucumber, scallions, raisins, parsley, pepper flakes, mint, cumin, oil and lemon juice. Season with salt and pepper. Serve at room temperature.

— *Makes four servings.*

Lemon Chicken, Hungarian Style

Cucumber Salad
★ Lemon Chicken, Hungarian Style
New Potatoes and Spring Vegetables

Those big roaster chicken breasts now becoming more widely available in markets were the inspiration for Lemon Chicken, Hungarian Style. The chicken cooks up naturally moist and juicy and is the perfect ingredient for a simply prepared dish such as this.

Serve the dish with a big bowl of tiny new potatoes that have been steamed, then tossed in parsley butter, and with a variety of spring vegetables for a meal that's as delicious as it is timely and easy to prepare. Cucumber salad, dressed with herb vinegar, would do nicely for that course.

★ Lemon Chicken, Hungarian Style

2 roaster chicken breasts or 3 broiler breasts
3 tablespoons butter, divided
1 cup strong chicken broth
1 tablespoon flour
1 teaspoon sugar
1 tablespoon lemon juice
1 teaspoon grated lemon rind
½ teaspoon dried tarragon
1 cup sour cream
Salt, pepper
3 slices bacon, fried dry, crumbled

• Skin and bone chicken breasts and cut into large cubes. Melt two tablespoons of butter in a large skillet and saute chicken cubes in butter for about five minutes or until chicken begins to firm and color.

• Add chicken broth to pan and cook five to 10 minutes, or until chicken is cooked through.

• Meanwhile, melt remaining butter in small skillet. Add flour and cook, stirring constantly, until mixture browns nicely.

• Drain cooked chicken, reserving broth. Stir broth into flour mixture in skillet with sugar, lemon juice, lemon rind and tarragon. Cook, stirring constantly, until mixture is hot and thickened. Stir in chicken cubes and sour cream and heat through, but do not boil or the sour cream will curdle. Season to taste with salt and pepper. Serve immediately, topped with crumbled bacon.

— *Makes four to six servings.*

TIPS/*LEMONS*

• To **extract the juice** from a reluctant lemon, microwave the lemon for a few seconds before squeezing. Don't overdo it. You don't want to boil the juice.

• If a recipe specifies **freshly grated lemon zest**, grate the lemon at the time you will be using it for best flavor and aroma.

• If you're using a lemon for **juice and zest**, grate the zest first then squeeze the juice.

• Use **lemon juice** in a recipe when you want lemon taste and tartness. Use **lemon rind** when you simply want the taste. Or blend some rind and juice to get the desired flavor.

• **Lemongrass**, popular with cooks in Southeast Asia, adds a lemony flavor and aroma to many dishes. The tropical grass is available fresh, frozen, dried or powdered. Fresh lemongrass can be stored in the refrigerator for several weeks.

Quick Country Captain

C hicken Country Captain, a curry-spiced dish, is a favorite with Southern cooks. Although recipes vary slightly, there are certain essential
ingredients including tomatoes, curry powder, thyme, currants and
almonds. Most of the recipes specify uncooked chicken parts, but we've made
the recipe faster to prepare by using strips of chicken breast.

Because the chicken has been trimmed of skin and fat, and because only a
small amount of fat is used in sauteing it and the vegetables (you'll use a
nonstick pan), this is an excellent dish for dieters. It would be delicious
served over plain steamed rice with lemon-buttered steamed cauliflower for
the vegetable.

★ Quick Country Captain

*2 large frying chicken breasts,
    skinned and boned*
Salt and pepper
1 tablespoon butter
1 tablespoon oil
1 medium onion, sliced
1 clove garlic, minced
1 green pepper, sliced into rings
1½ teaspoons curry powder
½ teaspoon dried thyme
1 can (1 pound) stewed tomatoes
3 tablespoons currants
1 tablespoon slivered almonds

• Cut chicken into long, thin strips. Season lightly with salt and pepper.
In medium skillet, heat butter. Saute chicken strips in butter until all
surfaces look white. Remove chicken from pan and keep warm.

• Heat oil in skillet and add onion, garlic and pepper slices. Saute until
onion and pepper begin to soften. Add curry powder and thyme, and saute a
minute or two longer. Add stewed tomatoes and stir to blend. Return

chicken to skillet. Cook a minute or two until chicken is cooked through. Stir in currants. Heat until currants plump. Sprinkle with almonds.

— *Makes four to six servings.*

★ Lemon Cauliflower

1 small head cauliflower
1 lemon, sliced
2 tablespoons lemon juice
2 tablespoons butter
1 teaspoon grated lemon rind
Salt and pepper

• Break cauliflower into florets. Arrange cauliflower and lemon slices in steamer and steam until cauliflower is crisp tender. Blend lemon juice, butter and lemon rind. Toss with steamed cauliflower and lemon slices. Add salt and pepper to taste. Serve immediately.

— *Makes six servings.*

Grilled Chicken Breasts
With Garlic Mayonnaise

★ **Antipasto Loaf**
★ **Grilled Chicken Breasts**
   With Garlic Mayonnaise
★ **Fried Spinach Leaves**
★ **Lemon-Parmesan Rice**

Almost anyone has time to give this easy party. The whole meal takes less than an hour to assemble, yet it looks festive and is affordable.

Start with an antipasto loaf that serves as appetizer, salad and bread. This colorful combination of fennel, olives, red onion, watercress, mozzarella, and cherry tomatoes is contained in a hollowed-out loaf of crusty French or Italian bread and sliced into individual portions at serving time.

For a chic new main course, offer sauteed or grilled boneless chicken breast with a sauce of fragrant garlic cream. And for a garnish that's delicious and different, surround the platter with a wreath of fried spinach leaves. That's right, fried spinach. Individual spinach leaves that have been washed and carefully dried (to minimize spattering) will fry in hot oil to the crispness of potato chips in a matter of seconds.

Lemon-Parmesan Rice and a confetti of sauteed strips of red and green peppers round out the entree, giving you a dinner plate filled with flavor and eye appeal. If you want to be slightly extravagant, use the new pecan rice available in fancy food stores. The unusual, nutty flavor makes this rice worth the premium price.

★ Antipasto Loaf

*2 jars (6½ ounces each) marinated
   artichoke hearts
2 cups fresh fennel slices
1 cup mixed green and black olives
12 cherry tomatoes, cut in half
1 medium red onion, cut into rings
½ pound mozzarella, cut into 1-inch cubes
A long, thin loaf of crusty bread
1 bunch watercress, washed
   and stems removed*

- Cut artichoke hearts in half. Toss fennel, olives, tomatoes, onion rings, cheese cubes and artichoke hearts with artichoke marinade.
- Slice bread horizontally to remove top crust. Carefully remove soft bread, leaving crust intact. Line inside of loaf with watercress, stem side down. Spoon fennel mixture into loaf. Pour any remaining dressing over top. Set aside while preparing rest of meal.
- At serving time, slice loaf on the diagonal into eight sections.

— *Makes eight servings.*

★ Grilled Chicken Breasts With Garlic Mayonnaise

4 large chicken breasts, boned,
*   skinned and halved*
Olive oil
1 large clove garlic, thinly sliced
1½ cups safflower oil, divided
1 egg
1 tablespoon fresh lemon juice
Salt and white pepper to taste
Fried Spinach Leaves (see recipe)

- Brush chicken breasts on both sides with olive oil. Set aside at room temperature while preparing mayonnaise.
- Cook garlic in one-quarter cup of the safflower oil over moderately high heat for about 30 seconds. Garlic should release flavor but should not brown. Remove garlic, and discard. Let oil cool to lukewarm.
- In a processor or blender, combine egg, lemon juice and garlic oil. Process until smooth and well-blended. With motor running, add remaining oil drop by drop until mixture begins to thicken, then in a steady, slow stream. Season to taste with salt and pepper. Add more juice if desired.
- Grill chicken 10 minutes per side. Season to taste with salt and pepper. At serving time, drizzle mayonnaise over warm chicken breasts. Garnish with Fried Spinach Leaves.

— *Makes eight servings.*

★ Fried Spinach Leaves

32 large spinach leaves, washed
*   and patted thoroughly dry*
Oil, for frying
Salt (optional)

• Choose the variety of spinach that has large, rather flat leaves. Such spinach is usually sold in bunches rather than bags. Wash carefully to remove any sand. Dry carefully to prevent spattering during frying. It helps, too, to have a spatter shield for your frying pan.
• Heat oil to 375 degrees. Fry spinach a few leaves at a time until leaves are crisp and translucent, no more than a few seconds. Drain on paper towels. Salt lightly if desired.
— *Makes enough for eight garnishes.*

★ Lemon-Parmesan Rice

2 cups long-grain rice
4 tablespoons (½ stick) butter
4 cups well-seasoned chicken broth
3 tablespoons freshly grated Parmesan cheese
Freshly grated rind of 1 lemon

• Saute rice in melted butter until rice looks opaque. Stir in chicken broth. Bring broth to boil, reduce heat, cover and cook for 15 minutes or until rice is tender. At serving time, stir in cheese and lemon rind.
— *Makes eight servings.*

Turkey With Tuna Mayonnaise

> ★ **Turkey With Tuna Mayonnaise**
> **Raw Vegetables**
> **Pita Bread**

Turkey with Tuna Mayonnaise is similar to vitello tonnato, a classic warm-weather dish from Italy.

The recipe would be a perfect use for leftover turkey, and if you have some from a freshly roasted bird (or in the freezer), you're in luck. If you don't, however, and don't want to heat the oven, poach either a turkey breast or legs (which are often bargain-priced) in broth until they're tender. Or use sliced turkey breast from the deli. Avoid bologna-like processed turkey, which is too salty for this use.

The recipe can be made at serving time or hours earlier. Take advantage of the good sauce by offering tomato wedges, green pepper rings, radishes and red onion rings as accompaniments. Pita bread would work well to scoop up vegetables, turkey and sauce.

★ Turkey With Tuna Mayonnaise

> *1 pound cooked turkey*
> *1 large can garbanzo beans, drained*
> *1 cup mayonnaise*
> *½ cup olive oil*
> *¼ cup lime juice*
> *1 can (6½ ounces) tuna in oil*
> *1 can flat anchovies*
> *Ripe olives, cocktail onions (for garnish)*

• Remove skin and bones from turkey if necessary. Slice neatly and arrange in serving dish, over well-drained garbanzo beans. In blender or processor, mix mayonnaise, oil and lime juice. Drain oil from tuna and anchovies, and discard oil. Blend tuna and four of the anchovies with mayonnaise mixture until smooth. (Reserve remaining anchovies for garnish.) Pour tuna mayonnaise over turkey. Garnish with reserved anchovies, olives and onions. Refrigerate until serving time.

• Note: To make recipe without processor or blender, mash drained tuna and anchovies well with a fork and add to remaining ingredients.

— *Makes four to six servings.*

Turkey Burgers Deluxe

Garden Lettuce
★ **Mustard Vinaigrette**
★ **Turkey Burgers Deluxe**
★ **Garlic and Anchovy Potatoes**
Fresh Peas

Ground turkey has all of the versatility of ground beef yet costs less and usually has lower fat content. If you dote on hamburger, you'll find that turkey, seasoned with salt, pepper, some finely chopped onion and, if desired, garlic, makes delicious patties.

Because the meat is so low in fat, you might want to cook it in a nonstick skillet with just a tiny bit of butter for flavor and browning. At serving time, add a dollop of sour cream and some chopped chives.

For a delightful early summer meal that can be made in less than an hour, serve the turkey burgers with Garlic and Anchovy Potatoes and a salad of garden lettuce served with a light Mustard Vinaigrette.

Fresh peas would make a good vegetable acccompaniment. Buy either the old-fashioned peas that need shelling or the newer types that cook in their own pods.

★ Turkey Burgers Deluxe

1 pound ground turkey
½ teaspoon salt
⅛ teaspoon pepper
1 small onion, chopped
1 small clove garlic, finely minced
1 teaspoon butter
¼ cup sour cream
1 teaspoon chopped chives

• Mix ground turkey with salt, pepper, onion and garlic. Shape into four large patties. Melt butter in skillet and brown patties on both sides. Cover and cook for 10 minutes or until patties are cooked through. Remove from pan and keep warm. Stir sour cream into pan to incorporate browned particles. Add chives. Taste and add additional salt and pepper if needed. Spoon sour cream mixture over patties and serve.

— *Makes four servings.*

★ Garlic and Anchovy Potatoes

12 small new potatoes
1 tablespoon virgin olive oil
2 anchovy filets, minced
1 small garlic clove, minced
Freshly ground pepper

• Steam potatoes until tender, and drain well. If you scrub them before cooking, they will not require peeling.

• Heat oil in skillet. Add anchovy filets and garlic and saute over medium heat for one minute. Add hot well-drained potatoes and cook, covered for three minutes, shaking pan to cook potatoes evenly. Season to taste with pepper. (Anchovies should provide enough salt).

— *Makes four servings.*

★ Mustard Vinaigrette

1 cup salad oil
⅓ cup wine vinegar
½ teaspoon salt
½ teaspoon pepper
1 teaspoon Dijon mustard

• Combine all ingredients in jar with tight-fitting lid. Shake vigorously. Shake before using.

— *Makes 1⅓ cups.*

Peking-Style Turkey

Melon With Lime or Ginger
Cucumber and Tomato Salad
★ Peking-Style Turkey
★ Sauce for Turkey
Rice
Stir-fry Zucchini

One of Peking's more famous dishes is lamb, marinated in a mixture of soy sauce and sherry, stir-fried with garlic and scallions and finished with a simple sweetened soy sauce.

But suppose you don't like, can't find or can't afford lamb? Then consider an updated version of the dish made with convenient turkey cutlets.

The dish lends itself nicely to Western-style meals. For a summer menu both appetizing and seasonal, begin with fresh ripe melon wedges served with a squeeze of lime or a dusting of powdered ginger. Add steamed white rice, a cucumber and tomato salad with a fresh herb vinaigrette, and stir-fried zucchini to which you've added a bit of garlic.

★ Peking-Style Turkey

1 pound thin turkey breast cutlets
1 teaspoon soy sauce
1 teaspoon sherry
Sauce (see recipe)
2 tablespoons corn oil
2 cloves garlic, sliced thinly
1 bunch scallions, trimmed, cut in long slivers
1 tablespoon chopped fresh ginger
Dash of sesame oil

• Cut cutlets into strips ½-inch wide. Place turkey in shallow bowl and sprinkle with soy sauce and sherry. Toss to coat well with liquids, and set aside for five minutes.

• Prepare sauce and set aside.

• Heat wok over high heat. Add oil and swirl to coat surface of pan. Add sliced garlic to hot oil, cooking just until garlic begins to color.

• Drain turkey of any residual marinade and add turkey to hot wok. Stir-fry until turkey begins to look cooked. Add sauce and scallions and ginger

and toss for a few seconds to cook scallions and absorb sauce. Mixture should look slightly dry. Remove to warmed serving platter and drizzle with sesame oil. Serve with steamed rice.
— *Makes four servings.*

★ Sauce for Turkey

½ teaspoon sugar
½ teaspoon red pepper flakes
1 teaspoon soy sauce
1 teaspoon sherry
1 teaspoon sesame oil

• Combine sauce ingredients. Use as directed in recipe above.

TIPS/*CHINESE COOKING*

• Americans are discovering that the Chinese have a variety of regional styles, each with distinctive dishes and seasonings. The **Cantonese** are China's most adventurous cooks. Cantonese cooking gave us crisp stir-fried vegetables, light sauces and bright flavors.

• **Fukien** province cooks specialize in distinctively seasoned river fish and seafood. Although Amoy, one of Fukien's major cities, makes excellent soy sauce, it is usually exported to other regions and used only sparingly in the region. Highly seasoned salt is sometimes used as a dip for the area's fried foods.

• Foods from **Hunan and Szechwan** are the most intensely flavored in all of China. Chili, garlic, onions, ginger and Szechwan peppercorns are favored seasonings.

• **Peking's** elegantly simple specialties include the famous Peking duck. Peking is unique among the provinces in that wheat flour breads and buns are popular there.

49

Seafood

Canned salmon is the starting point for this
New England-style meal. Pan-fried Salmon
Burgers are garnished with lemon and scallions.

Baked Fish With Oysters and Champagne

Watercress and Endive Salad
★ Baked Fish With Oysters
  and Champagne
Wild Rice
Stir-fry Snow Peas and Mushrooms

In addition to shaving a full hour from the cooking time for Baked Fish With Oysters and Champagne, the use of bottled clam broth gave its own sea-rich flavor to this elegant dish. Since the fairly salty broth was used both as the liquid for oven-poaching of the fish and as the basis for the sauce, additional salt was not required.

Be careful not to overcook the fish. Unless the filets are very thick, the cooking should be complete in just 10 minutes. Oysters, which are placed on top of the fish, cook along with them.

Because the sauce is rich, you might want to keep the rest of the meal fairly simple. And because the fish is flavorful but not particularly colorful, it would help to have a bright vegetable. A stir-fried combination of snow peas and mushrooms and some wild rice would do nicely.

For a salad, consider watercress and Belgian endive tossed with toasted walnuts and a simple vinaigrette.

★ Baked Fish With Oysters and Champagne

4 large filets of mild fish, such as
  flounder, fluke or sea bass
3 tablespoons softened butter
12 oysters, removed from shells,
  liquor reserved
White pepper to taste
1 bottle (8 ounces) clam broth
1 cup heavy cream
1 cup champagne or dry white wine
Salt (optional)

• With a sharp knife, make a few shallow, parallel cuts along the boned side of each filet to prevent fish from curling while cooking. Cuts should be about one inch apart. Spread most of the softened butter on the fish.

• With remaining butter, grease a large shallow baking dish and a square of parchment large enough to cover the dish. Place filets in dish, side by side. Place three oysters on each filet. Sprinkle with white pepper. Pour one-quarter cup of clam broth over fish and oysters. Cover with a parchment paper placed buttered-side down over the baking dish. This keeps the fish moist.

• Make sauce by boiling remaining clam broth, oyster liquor, cream and champagne in a saucepan until liquid is reduced to half the original volume. Bake fish in 375-degree oven for 10 minutes. When fish is cooked, set aside in a warm place. Pour liquid in baking dish into reduced cream mixture and cook over high heat for three minutes. Taste, adding salt and pepper if necessary.

• Spoon sauce over fish. Serve immediately.

— *Makes four servings.*

TIPS/*OYSTERS*

• If an **oyster** is open, even slightly, and it doesn't close tightly when handled, discard it. Dead oysters are unfit to eat.

• Live oysters can be **stored under refrigeration** for two or three days.

• **Opening an oyster** is easier if you first break off a piece of the thin end of the shell using a hammer. This will give you an opening into which to insert the oyster knife.

• Open a half-dozen oysters at a time by using **the microwave**. Place the scrubbed oysters in a single layer on a microwavable dish. Cover tightly and microwave for about two minutes.

Pan-Fried Porgy

> ★ **Warm Coleslaw**
> ★ **Pan-Fried Porgy**
>   **Warm Potato Chips**
>   **Biscuits**

L ike songbirds and wildflowers, porgies are among life's undervalued pleasures. The porgy is a relatively inexpensive small fish that's widely available. One fish makes a portion, and pan-frying it takes less than half an hour from start (dipping in cornmeal) to finish (adding a squeeze of lemon).

Don't let the market remove the dorsal (top) fin. When the fish is cooked, you can pull this long fin out with your hands, taking a row of small bones with it.

Do eat the skin. Cornmeal-coated and fried, it's crisp and delicious. Eat the porgy itself one side at a time, lifting the flesh off the bone carefully with a fork and turning the fish when you've finished the first side. That way, you shouldn't have any trouble getting boneless bites.

A porgy is a humble fish, so resist the urge to fancy it up through cooking or accompaniments. We like it best with warm potato chips (buy homestyle or freshly made chips, and warm them in the oven), Warm Coleslaw and those biscuits you buy in the refrigerated dough section of your supermarket.

★ Pan-Fried Porgy

1 porgy per serving
Cornmeal
Coarse salt
Freshly ground pepper
Vegetable oil for shallow frying
Fresh lemon

• Have porgies scaled and eviscerated. Wipe fish, and pat dry. Season cornmeal with salt and pepper and dredge each fish thoroughly with the seasoned cornmeal. In a small skillet, heat about one-half inch of oil. Fry fish five minutes, then turn and fry on second side for five more minutes, or until fish flakes easily with a fork. Serve with a squeeze of fresh lemon juice. Best when served immediately after cooking.

— *Makes one serving.*

★ Warm Coleslaw

1 small head young cabbage, shredded
1 small onion, peeled and chopped
1 small green pepper, seeded and chopped
4 egg yolks
½ teaspoon dry mustard
1 tablespoon sugar
1 tablespoon flour
1 tablespoon melted butter
1 cup tarragon vinegar
1 cup half-and-half
Salt and pepper to taste
¼ cup salad oil

• Prepare cabbage, onion and green pepper and combine. Make dressing by stirring together egg yolks, dry mustard, sugar, flour and butter. Stir in vinegar and half-and-half. Season and cook over medium heat, stirring constantly, until dressing is thick. Remove from heat, and beat in oil. Pour over cabbage mixture and serve immediately.

— *Makes six servings.*

Instant Fish

How long should you cook fish? If you start with a thin slice of tuna, sturgeon, sea bass or salmon, and you pound that slice until it's the thickness of a piece of flannel, you can cook it to just-right doneness in just seconds. And you don't even need a pan. The fish will cook perfectly on an ovenproof plate that you've heated under the broiler.

A simple Herb Butter added at serving time will add to the flavor of the finished dish and can also be made in minutes. Simply blend butter and lemon juice with a combination of fresh herbs, and spread some of the blended butter on the hot fish. Serve with fresh lemon wedges.

Put broth on to cook for couscous at the beginning of your preparation time, and the fluffy grain will be ready to serve with the fish. For a fast and easy fresh vegetable, grate carrots by blender or processor, and warm them in butter in a skillet for about five minutes.

★ Instant Fish

6 slices tuna, sturgeon, sea bass
  or salmon, each about 2 ounces
1 tablespoon butter, softened
Salt and pepper to taste
Herb Butter (see recipe)

• Preheat broiler. Place fish slices between sheets of wax paper, and pound them until they are about one-eighth inch thick.

• Place six heatproof plates in oven or under broiler. When plates are very hot, spread each slice of fish with half-teaspoon of butter. Season fish with salt and pepper, and place one slice of fish on each plate. Let stand in warm place for two minutes. Turn fish slices, and spread lightly with soft herb butter.

— *Makes six servings.*

★ Herb Butter

¼ pound (1 stick) soft butter
2 teaspoons lemon juice
1 tablespoon each: fresh parsley, chives
and tarragon

● Blend ingredients in blender or processor. Use as directed above. Cover and refrigerate remaining butter for use over fish, steak or vegetables.
— *Makes about one-half cup.*

TIPS/*SAUCES FOR FISH*

● **Dress up** simply cooked fish with a hot or cold sauce. For a zippy cold sauce, blend a half-cup of mayonnaise with two tablespoons grainy mustard, one tablespoon lemon juice and one teaspoon dill weed.

● Another **cold sauce**: Blend a half-cup of soy sauce with two cloves minced garlic and one tablespoon grated fresh ginger. Let stand 15 minutes, then strain out garlic and ginger. Add one tablespoon Chinese sesame oil to the strained soy and spoon over warm fish.

● For another **low-calorie sauce or dip** for fish, blend wasabi paste (Japanese green horseradish) into soy sauce. Use wasabi sparingly. It is very, very hot.

Tuna-Potato Pancakes

Spring Greens With Bacon Dressing   ★ **Tuna-Potato Pancakes**   ★ **Cucumber Mayonnaise**   **Steamed Asparagus Spears**

H ead for the pantry and a can of — don't raise that eyebrow — tuna. The fish that dieters eat by the carload, as is, seems to have been forgotten by modern cooks, and that's a pity. Canned tuna is a versatile food that blends well with many ingredients.

For this dinner, you'll be cooking some potatoes, but cooking them only until they soften slightly. You'll want them to be fairly firm so that they'll grate easily. (Save time and use a food processor with a shredding disk.)

Keep the tuna (we prefer chunk-style) in fairly large flakes and don't overhandle it. Shape the patties loosely, flattening them slightly so they'll brown nicely on both sides and will be cooked through the center.

After quick-frying the Tuna-Potato Pancakes in hot oil, drain them well on paper toweling and serve with easy Cucumber Mayonnaise (made with low-calorie mayonnaise if you're counting calories or your own homemade mayonnaise if you're not).

Easy and appropriate accompaniments of the season might be steamed asparagus spears and a salad of spring greens with bacon dressing.

★ Tuna-Potato Pancakes

2 large potatoes, peeled and cut
in large chunks
1 can (6½ ounces) chunk-style tuna
drained
6 scallions, coarsely chopped
¼ cup finely minced parsley
1 egg, lightly beaten
Salt and cayenne pepper to taste
Vegetable oil
Cucumber Mayonnaise (see recipe)

• Cover potatoes with salted water, and cook until fork penetrates easily but potatoes are still quite firm. Drain and let cool while draining and discarding water or oil from tuna.

• Grate potatoes coarsely using grater or grating blade of food processor. Gently mix grated potatoes, tuna, scallions, parsley, egg, salt and cayenne. Form into eight pancakes, shaping loosely but flattening slightly. In a large skillet, heat enough oil for shallow frying. Add pancakes. Do not overcrowd pan. Brown well on one side, then turn with slotted turner. Brown second side and remove pancakes from oil. Drain well on paper toweling. Serve with Cucumber Mayonnaise.

— *Makes four servings.*

★ Cucumber Mayonnaise

1 cup well-seasoned mayonnaise
1 teaspoon freshly grated lemon rind
½ cup finely chopped, seeded cucumber
Salt and pepper

• Combine ingredients. Taste and add salt and pepper if necessary.
— *Makes four servings.*

Monkfish, Shellfish Style

★ **Jennie's Celery Slaw**
★ **Monkfish, Shellfish Style**
★ **Oyster-Sauced Rice Noodles**

The resemblance in flavor of monkfish and crab is often noted. In most cases, however, the differences in size and shape between a standard fish filet or steak and crab chunks makes the substitution of moderately priced monk for expensive crab painfully obvious.

This dish — Monkfish, Shellfish Style — was developed for cooks in a hurry as well as those on a limited budget, and it manages to both look and taste like the higher-priced treat. The secret? Cut the fish into bite-size chunks.

It only takes a few minutes to saute the fish. At serving time, sprinkle it with chopped parsley, freshly grated lemon rind and a squeeze of fresh lemon juice. Stir the seasonings into the hot, buttery fish with salt and cayenne pepper to taste.

For an unusual but quickly prepared salad, slice celery thinly (use your processor if you own one), and serve with coleslaw dressing and a sprinkling of celery seed. An interesting starch to complement the fish is rice noodles with oyster sauce.

★ Monkfish, Shellfish Style

1 pound monkfish
Flour seasoned with salt, pepper, paprika
4 tablespoons butter, divided
1 tablespoon oil
1 clove garlic, minced
1 lemon
2 tablespoons chopped parsley
Salt, cayenne pepper to taste

• Cut fish into one-inch chunks. Coat fish lightly in seasoned flour. Melt three tablespoons butter with oil in large skillet. Add garlic and saute one minute. Add floured fish. Avoid crowding. Cook over high heat until fish chunks are lightly browned, about two to four minutes. Add remaining butter to pan. Grate lemon to get one tablespoon rind. Squeeze half of lemon over fish and add grated lemon rind with parsley, salt and cayenne. Heat, stirring, to blend. Serve fish with pan juices over top.

— *Makes four servings.*

★ Jennie's Celery Slaw

1 bunch celery, washed, leaves removed
1 cup mayonnaise
1 cup sour cream
1 teaspoon salt
1 tablespoon sugar (or to taste)
½ teaspoon pepper
2 teaspoons horseradish
Sprinkle of celery seeds

• Slice celery thinly. Make dressing by combining mayonnaise, sour cream, salt, sugar, pepper and horseradish. Combine celery and dressing with celery seeds. Adjust seasoning.

— *Makes four to six servings.*

★ Oyster-Sauced Rice Noodles

½ pound dried rice noodles
2 quarts boiling water
Chinese oyster sauce (to taste)
3 scallions, finely chopped
1 teaspoon chopped fresh coriander

• Drop rice noodles into boiling water and soak until they soften, about 30 seconds. Drain well and toss with oyster sauce and scallions. Garnish with fresh coriander, if desired.

• Note: Rice noodles and oyster sauce are available in Asian food markets. Fresh coriander is available in Asian and Hispanic food markets.

— *Makes four servings.*

San Francisco Ginger Sole

Tomato and Asparagus Salad
★ Broccoli and Cheese Bisque
★ San Francisco Ginger Sole
Instant Couscous

San Francisco Ginger Sole is an excellent diet choice in that it contains only one tablespoon of butter and one of cornstarch. A small amount of dry white wine adds flavor, but calories cook away. The real excitement of the dish is provided by two tablespoons of peeled fresh ginger shavings and a small amount of lime juice.

Even in winter, there are fresh foods to fill your meals with sunshiny flavor. Broccoli, that popular green vegetable, is available year-round, but is especially attractive in the cold-weather months when other vegetable choices are limited. Serve hearty Broccoli and Cheese Bisque as a first course, and you'll need a minimum of extras with the entree. We'd suggest buttered instant couscous (available at gourmet food shops) to absorb the flavorful sauce from the fish dish and, for color, a cherry tomato and asparagus salad with vinaigrette dressing.

★ Broccoli and Cheese Bisque

2 large leeks, cleaned and sliced
¼ pound mushrooms, washed and sliced
2 tablespoons butter
2 tablespoons flour
1½ cups chicken broth
½ cup broccoli, chopped
½ cup milk
½ cup shredded mild cheese

• In large pan, saute leeks and mushrooms in butter 10 minutes or until tender but not brown. Add flour and cook, stirring, until flour is incorporated. Remove from heat and blend in broth. Return to heat. Cook, stirring until thickened and smooth. Add broccoli. Reduce heat and simmer 20 minutes or until broccoli is tender. Blend in milk and cheese. Simmer until heated through and cheese is melted.

— *Makes four servings.*

★ San Francisco Ginger Sole

4 large filets of sole, about 1½ pounds
4 large shrimp, peeled and deveined
1 cup chicken broth
¼ cup dry white wine
2 tablespoons peeled fresh ginger shavings
    (use vegetable parer)
2 teaspoons lime juice
1 tablespoon cornstarch
1 tablespoon water
1 tablespoon butter

• Roll sole filets around shrimp, securing with toothpicks. In saucepan, bring broth, wine, ginger and lime juice to simmering. Add sole; cover and simmer gently about five minutes or until sole flakes. Transfer fish to heated serving dish; remove toothpicks. Mix cornstarch and water. Add to broth, stirring over medium heat until thickened. Stir in butter. Serve over sole.

— *Makes four servings.*

TIPS/*FISH AND MORE*

• To be sure that a **fish is fresh**, look for firm, fresh eyes that are still convex and gills that are bright red. Many cooks insist on buying whole fish rather than filets and steaks because the latter make it impossible to look for these telltale signs.

• **Chinese gourmets** eat the whole fish, prizing the delicate flavor and firm texture of the cheeks and tongue.

• That so many fish and seafood recipes contain **ginger** is no accident. Chinese cooks have learned that the lively seasoning brightens seafood flavors and makes everything taste fresher.

• When incorporating **cheese** into a mixture such as Broccoli and Cheese Bisque, add the cheese at the last minute and keep the heat to a simmer. High heat and long cooking will toughen cheese.

Zuppa di Pesce

★ **Zuppa di Pesce**
★ **Pasta Primavera Salad**
   Peasant Bread

A friend presents you with some freshly caught fish and you have never cooked fish before. Moreover, you want to use the fish while it's at its peak and you don't have time to fuss. The solution? Fish soup.

Many cooks are surprised to learn that excellent fish soups can be prepared from scratch in just a few minutes. Zuppa di Pesce, from northern Italy, is just such a soup. The recipe requires no unusual ingredients and yet is absolutely delicious. Serve the soup hot with peasant bread and butter.

For a late summer meal almost sure to satisfy, follow the soup with Pasta Primavera Salad made with macaroni in your favorite shape, plus broccoli, zucchini, asparagus, mushrooms, onions and cherry tomatoes in a creamy dressing flavored with Parmesan cheese.

★ Pasta Primavera Salad

3 cups uncooked macaroni
1 cup broccoli florets
1 cup sliced zucchini
1 cup asparagus, cut into 1-inch pieces
1 cup sliced mushrooms
½ cup chopped onions
¼ cup vegetable oil
2 cups cherry tomatoes, cut in halves
2 tablespoons minced parsley
¼ cup Parmesan cheese, grated
½ cup creamy Italian dressing
¼ cup milk

• Cook macaroni according to package directions; drain well. Saute broccoli, zucchini, asparagus, mushrooms and onions in oil until tender but not browned. Add tomatoes and parsley; simmer about five minutes.

• Combine cheese, dressing and milk in a small bowl; mix until smooth. Combine macaroni, vegetable mixture and dressing in large serving bowl; toss lightly until ingredients are blended. Serve garnished with parsley and Parmesan cheese if desired.

• Note: Short-cut pasta shapes such as elbows, rotini, shells, rings, rigatoni and mostaccioli can be used interchangeably in this recipe.

— *Makes four to six servings.*

★ Zuppa di Pesce

2 tablespoons olive oil
1 clove garlic, finely chopped
1 onion, peeled and chopped
1 tablespoon chopped parsley
2 cups cold water
1½ pounds fish, cut in 2-inch pieces
Salt, pepper

• Heat oil in heavy pot. Add garlic, onion and parsley, and saute until onion softens. Add water, fish, salt and pepper. Bring to boil and then immediately lower heat to simmer. Cook 10 minutes or until fish is done.

— *Makes four servings.*

Salmon Burgers

Red Cabbage Slaw
★ **Salmon Burgers**
★ **Lemon Sour Cream Sauce**
Potatoes With Dill Butter
Peas

Canned salmon? When a friend's New England-born mother told a dinner crowd that she swore by the stuff, some in the group sniffed disdainfully. But even though salmon in a can lacks the delicate texture and flavor of fresh-poached salmon, the convenient pantry-shelf form of the fish has many delicious uses.

Casserole mixtures of canned salmon have always been popular, but we like the simple goodness of Salmon Burgers. What's more, a meal based on this easy recipe can be prepared in less than 30 minutes, making it ideal for modern cooks in a hurry. Drained canned salmon, egg, toasted bread crumbs and chopped scallions go into the burgers. An accompanying sauce is made from sour cream, lemon juice, lemon rind and sugar. Serve the pan-fried burgers with Lemon Sour Cream Sauce, fresh lemon wedges and fresh scallions. For accompaniments in a New England mood, offer tiny boiled potatoes with fresh dill butter, peas and a slaw of chopped red cabbage with a hint of vinegar blended in the mayonnaise dressing.

★ Salmon Burgers

---

1 can (16 ounces) salmon
1 egg, slightly beaten
1 cup bread crumbs,
    made from toasted bread
½ cup chopped scallions
Salt, pepper
3 tablespoons butter
Lemon Sour Cream Sauce (see recipe)
1 bunch scallions, trimmed
Lemon wedges

• Drain salmon, reserving liquid. With fork, break salmon into small pieces. Stir in beaten egg, bread crumbs and chopped scallions. Add salt and pepper to taste. (The salmon will be fairly salty, so be conservative with salt.) Mixture should be easy to shape into patties. If too dry, moisten with some of the reserved salmon liquid.

• Shape mixture into six equal-size patties. Heat butter in skillet large enough to hold all six patties without crowding. When butter begins to sizzle, add patties and brown well on both sides. Serve with Lemon Sour Cream Sauce and additional scallions and, if desired, lemon wedges.

— *Makes six servings.*

★ Lemon Sour Cream Sauce

1 cup sour cream
2 tablespoons fresh lemon juice
1 teaspoon freshly grated lemon rind
½ teaspoon sugar

• Combine all ingredients. Allow to stand a few minutes to blend flavors before serving.

— *Makes enough for six Salmon Burgers.*

Salmon Fritters

Iceberg Wedges
★ **Salmon Fritters**
★ **Fried Shoestring Potatoes**
Broccoli

Salmon Fritters may sound like something that takes time and effort to prepare, but the delicious fish nuggets need less than a half-hour to go from mixing bowl to table.

Since you already have cooking oil hot to cook the fritters, round out the meal with Fried Shoestring Potatoes (made from scratch if you have the time, otherwise use frozen potatoes). Keep the vegetable something simple like broccoli, sold frozen in plastic bags that let you use as much or as little as you need.

For a sensational salad that couldn't be easier to make, top crisp wedges of iceberg lettuce with a dressing made of mayonnaise to which you've added imported soy sauce and chopped ripe olives. Let your own taste be the judge of how much soy to use.

★ Salmon Fritters

1 can (7¾ ounces) salmon
Milk
1 cup biscuit mix
1 egg, slightly beaten
1 teaspoon lemon juice
¼ cup finely chopped celery
2 tablespoons finely chopped green pepper
2 tablespoons finely chopped onion
1 tablespoon minced parsley
½ teaspoon seasoned salt
Oil for deep-frying
Lemon wedges
Seafood or tartar sauce

• Drain and flake salmon, reserving liquid. Add milk to salmon liquid to make one-half cup. Add liquid to biscuit mix along with egg and lemon juice. Blend in salmon, chopped vegetables, parsley and seasoned salt.

Drop batter by spoonfuls into oil for deep-frying heated to 375 degrees. Fry until golden brown on both sides, about three minutes. Drain on paper towels. Serve with lemon wedges and seafood or tartar sauce.
— *Makes four servings.*

★ Fried Shoestring Potatoes

3 large potatoes
Oil for deep-frying
Salt

• Peel potatoes and cut into strips. Let stand in cold water for 30 minutes. Dry thoroughly. Place dried potatoes in frying basket. Lower basket into hot oil (375 degrees) and cook until potatoes rise to top of oil and brown.
• Remove basket from fryer and let excess oil drain into fryer. Turn potatoes out onto absorbent toweling and sprinkle with salt. Serve hot.
— *Makes four servings.*

TIPS/*DEEP-FRYING*

• **Oils** suitable for deep-frying include corn, cottonseed, peanut, soybean or safflower. Never fill the fryer more than half-full of oil. There should be room for the oil to bubble without spilling over.

• Always **strain oil** before reusing it for deep-frying.

• If you're frying fish and potatoes for one meal, fry the potatoes first. Oil **will absorb some flavors** from the food, so always fry the milder-flavored food first.

• To **prevent spattering**, dry potatoes thoroughly with paper towels before frying.

• **Baking potatoes** are best for frying.

Slightly Extravagant Crab Cakes

★ **Chunky Guacamole**
  Coleslaw
★ **Slightly Extravagant Crab Cakes**
★ **Pan-Fried Potatoes With Sage**
  Asparagus Spears

At the seafood store, the special crab meat was half the price of lump crab. Flavor's the same, said the young man behind the counter. The only difference is in the size of the pieces. If you don't need big pieces (as you would in crab imperial, for example), don't buy them, he said.

The man was right. The crab shreds were as sweet as any super-expensive backfin lumps and just right for our Slightly Extravagant Crab Cakes.

For color, the meal could begin with guacamole with red pepper strips for dipping. Asparagus spears and Pan-Fried Potatoes With Sage would be appealing accompaniments. For a salad, offer traditional coleslaw.

★ Slightly Extravagant Crab Cakes

1 pound cooked crab meat

6 tablespoons mayonnaise

2 teaspoons grated lemon rind

2 tablespoons finely chopped or grated onion

2 tablespoons finely chopped parsley

Salt and cayenne pepper to taste

1 large egg

1 tablespoon fresh lemon juice

1 cup fine dry bread crumbs

4 tablespoons clarified butter

Lemon wedges (optional)

Caper mayonnaise (optional)

• Sort through crab meat, picking out and discarding any cartilage or shell pieces. Combine mayonnaise, lemon rind, onion and parsley, and gently mix into crab. Season mixture with salt and cayenne to taste.

• At this point, either refrigerate mixture, covered, for an hour to firm, or shape immediately into eight cakes no more than one-half inch thick. (For

70

hors d'oeuvres, shape into walnut-size balls, then flatten into cakes.)

• Lightly beat egg with lemon juice. Dip crab cakes into beaten egg and then into bread crumbs to coat evenly. Place crumb-coated crab cakes on a sheet of wax paper or plastic wrap.

• Heat butter in large skillet; don't allow to brown. Saute crab cakes in hot butter until nicely browned on both sides. Remove to heated platter. Serve with fresh lemon wedges and mayonnaise to which you've added drained capers to taste.

— *Makes four entree servings or about 16 hors d'oeuvres.*

★ Chunky Guacamole

1 large ripe avocado
Salt to taste
2 tablespoons chopped onion
½ teaspoon finely chopped
  fresh hot green chili
¼ cup chopped tomato
2 sprigs fresh cilantro, finely chopped
1 tablespoon lime juice
1 sweet red pepper, cut into strips

• Halve the avocado by cutting from stem to flower end, around the pit. Twist halves in opposite direction to loosen pit. Scoop out pit. Scrape pulp from skin and mash roughly with a spoon.

• Blend in remaining ingredients. Set aside for a few minutes to blend flavors then serve with sweet red pepper strips.

— *Makes four servings.*

★ Pan-Fried Potatoes With Sage

2 large boiled potatoes, sliced
1 small onion, sliced
2 tablespoons olive oil
3 fresh sage leaves, minced
  or 1 teaspoon dried sage, crumbled
Salt, pepper to taste

• Saute potatoes and onion in hot oil until potato pieces begin to brown. Add sage with salt and pepper. Cover, turn heat to low, let potatoes continue cooking for five minutes, tossing occasionally. Remove cover, turn heat to high, and let potatoes get crusty.

— *Makes four servings.*

Crab a la Russe

C rab meat and caviar go together in a seafood successor to beef stroganoff that has the same appealing flavors of dill, sour cream and mushroom, yet is lighter and easier to prepare.

Although the caviar garnish is optional, it is recommended for the lively color that the big red-orange salmon eggs give the dish. Buckwheat, a grain that is better known in Europe, makes noodles with an interesting, rather nutty flavor that are delicious with the crab combination. But the noodles can be hard to find, so if you can't locate them, good commercial (or, better yet, homemade) egg noodles will do nicely.

For a vegetable accompaniment, serve something with bright color and firm texture, like buttered green beans, lightly cooked to leave them bright and snappy. Add another flourish of color to the meal with a salad of ripe tomato slices in a garlic vinaigrette.

★ Crab a la Russe

1 pound lump crab meat

2 tablespoons butter

1 medium onion, sliced

½ pound fresh mushrooms, sliced

¾ cup sour cream

¼ cup dry white wine

1 tablespoon chopped fresh dill

1 teaspoon grated fresh lemon rind

Salt and pepper to taste

8 ounces buckwheat or egg noodles,
    cooked and buttered

Salmon caviar (optional)

• Carefully sort through crab meat, picking out any shell bits. Set crab aside while sauce is being prepared.

• Heat butter in large skillet to melt. In hot butter, saute onion and mushrooms until lightly browned. Stir in sour cream, wine and dill. Cook

72

over medium heat for five minutes to blend flavors. Cream should not be allowed to boil. Gently stir in lemon rind and crab meat, being careful not to break up large pieces of crab. Add salt and pepper. When crab and sauce are warmed through, serve over buttered buckwheat or egg noodles. If desired, sprinkle with salmon caviar for garnish.

• Note: Buckwheat noodles are available in some fresh-pasta or health food stores. Salmon caviar was chosen for its bright orange color. If desired, other caviars could be substituted.

— *Makes four to six servings.*

TIPS/*CRAB*

• By tradition, certain crab recipes are made only with a designated variety of crab. Crab Louis, for example, calls for the **Dungeness crab** found on America's West Coast. Maryland crab cakes would be made with Atlantic blue crabs as would Charleston's she-crab soup.

• **Stone crab claws** are a Southern delicacy. The crabs with the black-tipped claws are harvested from Texas to the Carolinas but are most abundant in Florida. In the interest of conservation, fishermen remove one claw from each crab caught and return the crab to the water where it will regenerate a new claw in time.

• **Lump crab** consists of large nuggets of body meat, and this premium-price product goes into special occasion recipes such as crab a la Russe as well as crab cocktails and salads. Backfin crab consists of smaller pieces of meat from the body of the crab. Least expensive is claw meat, which lacks the even white color of lump or backfin but is suitable for dishes where appearance is less important.

Scalloped Oysters

> Orange-Grape Salad
> ★ Honey-Lime Salad Dresssing
> ★ Scalloped Oysters
> ★ Zucchini Italienne

Oysters are always in season when it comes to dishes that cook quickly, yet highly satisfy the appetite. Scalloped Oysters is an old-fashioned combination of bread crumbs, oysters, chopped vegetables, butter, cream and oyster liquor that is surprisingly flavorful. It's the sort of dish that does best with tomato-sauced zucchini and a lively salad featuring orange slices and grapes in a honey-lime dressing.

★ Scalloped Oysters

2 cups dried bread crumbs
⅓ cup butter, melted
2 dozen medium oysters
2 tablespoons minced parsley
½ cup chopped celery
Salt, pepper
½ cup cream
¼ cup oyster liquor

• Mix bread crumbs and butter. In greased shallow pan, place layers of crumbs, oysters, parsley and celery. Season with salt and pepper. Repeat layers until all those ingredients are used. Pour cream and liquor over top. Bake at 350 degrees for 20 minutes or until browned and bubbling.
— *Makes six servings.*

★ Zucchini Italienne

6 small zucchini, about 1½ pounds
2 tablespoons butter or margarine
1 cup meatless spaghetti sauce
¼ cup grated Parmesan cheese

• Slice zucchini. Melt butter and saute zucchini for five minutes. Add spaghetti sauce, cover and simmer 10 minutes to blend flavors. Sprinkle with Parmesan cheese and serve.

— *Makes six servings.*

★ Honey-Lime Salad Dressing

½ cup vegetable oil
½ teaspoon grated lime peel
Juice of 2 limes
½ teaspoon dry mustard
¼ cup honey
Salt
¼ teaspoon paprika
⅛ teaspoon white pepper

• Blend ingredients well. Refrigerate until serving time. Serve over orange slices and seedless green grapes on well-washed romaine.

— *Makes about ¾ cup.*

Mussel Stew

Avocado With Mustard Vinaigrette
★ **Mussel Stew**
Shell-Shaped Corn Muffins

M ussels open very quickly. Steam them in wine or water to which you've added a few chopped shallots and remove the mussels as they open. Put them aside while you make the buttery base for this delicious mussel stew.

You could serve the stew with traditional oyster crackers or you could be more imaginative and offer seashell-shaped corn sticks. Several attempts to develop the pretty miniatures using favorite corn bread recipes and a borrowed Madeleine pan were failures. The batter stuck in the indentations of the pan every time. What finally worked was spraying the pans with commercial pan spray and making the muffins using corn muffin mix. Batter made from a box of the mix filled all of the cavities in the Madeleine pan. If you lack such a pan, make regular corn bread, muffins or sticks.

This meal could stand a substantial appetizer salad. Consider avocado slices sprinkled with chopped nuts and tossed gently with mustard vinaigrette.

★ Mussel Stew

---

3 pounds mussels
1½ cups white wine or water
3 shallots, minced
3 tablespoons butter or margarine
2 tablespoons flour
1 small clove garlic, minced
½ teaspoon curry powder
3 cups warm milk
1 cup heavy cream
Salt, pepper to taste

• Scrub mussels, removing as much of the beards as possible. In large pan with cover, steam mussels in wine or water to which you have added the minced shallots. As mussels open, remove from cooking pan and set aside. When they have opened and cooled enough to handle, remove remaining portions of beard.

• Strain cooking liquid and reserve one cup. Heat butter in saucepan. Stir in flour, garlic and curry. Cook, stirring, for a minute or two. Slowly stir in milk and one cup of strained mussel cooking liquid. Heat, stirring until mixture thickens slightly. Add heavy cream and mussels and heat until mussels are heated through. Taste and adjust seasoning.

— *Makes four servings.*

To make **Shell-Shaped Corn Muffins**: Mix one 8½-ounce package of corn muffin mix with egg and milk according to package directions. Spray Madeleine pan with commercial pan spray according to directions on spray can. Fill shell-shaped depressions in pan with about a tablespoon of muffin batter. Batter should be sufficient to fill all the indentations in the pan. Bake in preheated 350-degree oven for 10 to 15 minutes or until lightly browned. Makes 12 muffins.

TIPS/*MUSSELS*

● A **wire brush**, like those used by house painters, makes quick and easy work of scrubbing mussels.

● To **cleanse mussels** of sand, soak them in salt water (⅓ cup salt per gallon of water) for 15 minutes. Rinse and repeat several times.

● Many of the mussels sold today are cleaned and ready to use, but if the mussels you buy still have the **beards** attached, remove the beards just before cooking and not before.

● If a mussel feels extra heavy, it is probably **filled with silt** and should be discarded. Discard open (dead) mussels as well.

Marinated Scallop Salad

Chicken Curry Soup
★ Marinated Scallop Salad
Crusty Bread

The recipe for Marinated Scallop Salad starts with coarsely chopped, uncooked sea scallops, or the smaller bay scallops left whole. The acid in the marinade firms the scallops and changes their texture in the same way that cooking does. No heat is required. Everything can be assembled in minutes, but the salad needs at least four hours, preferably overnight, to be at its flavorful best.

We like the salad with crusty bread as a lunch or light supper preceded by cream of chicken soup spiked with curry and sprinkled with coconut.

★ Marinated Scallop Salad

1 pound scallops
3 tablespoons lime juice
2 tablespoons white wine vinegar
3 tablespoons olive oil
3 sprigs fresh thyme or ⅛ teaspoon dried
6 leaves fresh basil, minced
2 tablespoons finely minced parsley
1 bunch scallions, finely chopped
¼ teaspoon sugar
Salt, pepper to taste
Shredded iceberg lettuce

• Chop sea scallops coarsely and set aside. If using bay scallops, leave the scallops whole. In glass bowl, mix lime juice, vinegar, oil, thyme, basil, parsley, scallions, sugar, salt and pepper. Add scallops and toss gently to mix thoroughly. Cover with plastic wrap and refrigerate at least four hours or overnight, stirring occasionally.

• Serve chilled over iceberg lettuce.

— *Makes four to six servings.*

Vodka-Steamed Scallops

★ **Vodka-Steamed Scallops**
Kasha
Steamed Snow Peas

Although there are special utensils designed for steaming (including microwave steamers), no special equipment is needed to produce Vodka-Steamed Scallops.

The cooking can be done using a pot with a good lid fitted with an ovenproof dish large enough to hold the scallops and seasonings but small enough to allow the steam to circulate around the edges of the dish. You will also need a small rack to raise the dish over the boiling water in the bottom of the pot. (Lacking such a rack, you might use a tuna fish can that has had both top and bottom removed with a can opener.)

Steaming is a quick-cooking method that busy cooks sometimes overlook. Steamed vegetables are brighter and crisper than immersion-cooked equivalents. Steamed fish and shellfish keep their delicate flavors and textures, yet absorb the flavors of any added seasonings nicely.

Kasha, the chewy buckwheat grain, and steamed snow peas would make attractive accompaniments.

★ Vodka-Steamed Scallops

1 pound bay scallops
1 tablespoon vodka
½ teaspoon cornstarch
1 tablespoon minced ginger
¼ cup chopped scallions
1 tablespoon chopped fresh coriander
1 tablespoon peanut oil
2 cloves garlic, crushed
1 tablespoon soy sauce

• In a large bowl, toss scallops with vodka and cornstarch. Place scallops in bowl that is suitable for steaming. Top with ginger, scallions and coriander. Steam over boiling water for five minutes. While scallops steam, heat oil in a small skillet. Add garlic and reduce heat, cooking until the garlic just begins to brown. Remove garlic. Add soy sauce, blending well. Pour garlic- and soy-flavored oil over cooked scallops. Serve immediately over hot kasha.

— *Makes four servings.*

Sea Captain's Salad

★ **Green Pea Salad**
★ **Dill Vinaigrette**
★ **Sea Captain's Salad**
★ **Fresh Tomato Sauce**

Summer party food should be visually appealing, which is why this plan features Sea Captain's Salad. The dish looks and tastes expensive in that it contains lobster in the dressing and is garnished with two bright red lobster claws. But the secret is that one small lobster, two pounds of mussels and a dozen clams will make enough of this salad for eight servings. If you buy the lobster on the way home from a New England visit, as I did, you could find that your party entree doesn't cost much more than $1 a serving.

We like a bright Green Pea Salad as an accompaniment. Don't cook the peas. They're just right as they come from defrosting. If you don't count defrosting time, the salad should take about 10 minutes to fix.

★ Sea Captain's Salad

1 lobster (the biggest you can afford)
12 littleneck clams
2 pounds mussels
1 pound medium-size shell macaroni
1 cup good mayonnaise
1 recipe Fresh Tomato Sauce (see recipe)
Salt, pepper

- Steam lobster, clams and mussels separately. Set aside to cool.
- Cook shell macaroni al dente following directions on the package. While macaroni cooks, blend mayonnaise and Fresh Tomato Sauce.
- Remove half of the mussels and clams from their shells and the lobster meat from the lobster tail. Shred lobster tail meat and add to tomato mayonnaise dressing. Reserve lobster claws and remaining clams and mussels in their shells for garnish.
- Drain pasta and cool slightly under running water. In large bowl, toss slightly warm pasta with clams and mussels that have been removed from shells and with lobster dressing. Cover with plastic wrap and refrigerate. Refrigerate in-shell clams, mussels and lobster claws separately.
- At serving time, taste and adjust seasoning, adding more salt and pepper and more mayonnaise, if necessary. Place pasta on platter and garnish with lobster claws (cracked for easy eating), in-shell clams and mussels.

— *Makes eight servings.*

★ Fresh Tomato Sauce

5 ripe tomatoes, peeled, seeds removed
3 to 4 tablespoons fresh lemon juice
2 cloves garlic, minced
½ teaspoon salt
½ cup fresh basil leaves

• Chop tomatoes coarsely. Drain to remove any excess juice. Add lemon juice, garlic and salt. Chop basil leaves, and add to tomato mixture. Use over hot pasta or as directed in dressing for Sea Captain's Salad.
— *Makes about 1½ cups.*

★ Green Pea Salad

3 packages frozen peas, defrosted
2 large cucumbers, peeled
2 bunches scallions
Dill Vinaigrette (see recipe)

• Drain defrosted peas to remove any excess water. (Do not cook them.) Cut cucumbers in quarters lengthwise. Remove seeds and slice thickly. Trim scallions and chop coarsely. Toss peas with cucumbers, scallions and Dill Vinaigrette.
— *Makes eight servings.*

★ Dill Vinaigrette

½ cup fresh lemon juice
½ cup olive oil
½ teaspoon salt
Pepper
1 teaspoon sugar
3 tablespoons chopped fresh dill or mint

• Combine lemon juice, olive oil, salt and pepper. Beat well to blend. Add sugar and dill or mint.
— *Makes about one cup.*

Easy Seafood Stew

★ **Broiled Brie**
Artichoke Hearts
★ **Easy Seafood Stew**
Italian Bread

While you put together an excellent seafood stew, your friends can nibble on Broiled Brie you've topped with almonds and butter and served with an assortment of crackers.

Salad? Just open a jar of marinated artichoke hearts. Chop the hearts into quarters and toss them, with a few sliced fresh mushrooms and the marinating liquid, with crisp romaine. Sprinkle well with grated Parmesan cheese, freshly grated if you have the time.

Serve a big basket of warm Italian bread to mop up the excellent liquid in the stew.

★ Easy Seafood Stew

1 tablespoon olive oil
1 large onion, peeled and chopped
2 large cloves garlic, minced
3 cups spaghetti sauce
1¾ cups strong chicken broth
1 cup water
½ cup white wine
1 bay leaf
1 teaspoon thyme
¼ teaspoon fennel seeds
1 pound fish (whitefish or other mild fish)
1 pound scallops
½ pound medium shrimp, peeled, deveined
1 dozen littleneck clams in shells, scrubbed

• In five-quart Dutch oven, heat oil. Saute onion and garlic until onion is tender. Stir in spaghetti sauce, broth, water, wine, seasonings. Heat to boiling. Reduce heat and simmer 20 minutes. Cut fish into large chunks and add with shellfish. Cover and simmer until clam shells open, about seven minutes. Discard bay leaf and serve.

— *Makes six servings.* 82

★ Broiled Brie

4½ ounces Brie cheese
2 tablespoons unsalted butter
¼ cup toasted almonds, chopped
1 tablespoon brandy

• Broil Brie three to four inches from broiler until soft and warm, about two to three minutes. Melt butter, stir in remaining ingredients and blend. Pour over cheese. Serve with crackers.

— *Makes four to six servings.*

TIPS/*BRIE*

• **Brie** originated in France centuries ago. The cheese is made from whole, skim or partially skim cow's milk. Brie-type cheeses are also made in America and other countries.

• Brie is often shipped before it is completely **ripened**. Many cheese retailers finish ripening the cheese in their own cellars. A whole Brie will ripen more quickly than a wedge.

• Because the cheese is **perishable**, Brie should be kept refrigerated.

• Brie and **Camembert** are similar in appearance. Although they have different flavors and aromas, one is often substituted for the other.

Quick Seafood Salad

Tossed Salad
★ Parmesan Salad Dressing
★ Quick Seafood Salad
★ Bruschette

C alling a recipe with 15 ingredients quick may sound like a mistake. Check through our Quick Seafood Salad formula, however, and you'll see that virtually everything for this summer party dish could be assembled with ease from a reasonably well-stocked pantry. The exceptions, of course, are the fresh sea scallops and frozen shrimp.

Small shrimp were chosen for this dish because they blend nicely with the scallop pieces. Buy fresh, in-shell shrimp, and you'll spend an hour cleaning and deveining. Good-quality frozen shrimp, on the other hand, can be purchased ready to cook.

An inexpensive variation of the recipe can be made by substituting a pound of squid for one pound of the scallops. If you do, though, be prepared to clean the squid, a messy but fast and easy process once you master it.

To clean squid: Separate the body tube from the tentacle portion by pulling apart. Cut off the tentacles close to the eyes. Rub off as much of the skin as will come off. Chop tentacles into one-inch pieces. From inside the body tube, remove and discard what feels like a piece of flexible plastic. Rub off the thin skin that covers body tube. Squeeze tube to remove any milky residue that might remain. Cut tube into rings half an inch wide.

To cook squid for Quick Seafood Salad, use the liquid in which the scallops have been cooked. Cook for one minute after the liquid comes to a boil. Squid are done when they turn white. Don't overcook or squid will be tough. Remove from liquid and set aside to cool. Use cooking liquid to cook shrimp.

Bruschette, the original garlic bread, would be perfect with the salad. You might also want to add a big green tossed salad with Parmesan dressing.

★ Parmesan Salad Dressing

¼ cup freshly grated Parmesan cheese
½ cup extra-virgin olive oil
2 tablespoons lemon juice
Salt, freshly ground pepper

● Place ingredients in a small bottle and shake well to blend. Serve over crisp fresh greens.

— *Makes enough for several salads.*

★ Quick Seafood Salad

2 pounds sea scallops or 1 pound
sea scallops and 1 pound squid
¼ teaspoon hot pepper flakes
1 large bay leaf
4 stems fresh parsley
Salt and freshly ground black pepper
½ cup dry white wine
1 pound small frozen shrimp, defrosted
½ cup olive oil
3 tablespoons fresh lemon juice
1 tablespoon red wine vinegar
2 cloves garlic, minced
¼ cup finely minced parsley
6 scallions, chopped coarsely
Sweet red pepper rings for garnish

● Cut each large sea scallop into four pieces. Place scallops in saute pan. Season with hot pepper, bay leaf, parsley stems, salt and black pepper. Add white wine and enough water to cover. Bring to a boil, uncovered, and reduce heat immediately. After one minute, remove scallops from cooking liquid with slotted spoon, and set aside to cool.

● Return cooking liquid to a boil and add shrimp. When liquid boils again, reduce heat immediately. After one minute, remove shrimp from cooking liquid with slotted spoon, and set aside to cool.

● When scallops and shrimp are cool, toss with olive oil, lemon juice, wine vinegar, garlic, minced parsley and scallions. Taste and adjust seasonings, adding more red pepper and salt if desired. Can be served immediately or refrigerated several hours or overnight. Garnish with sweet red pepper rings, if desired.

— *Makes six to eight servings.*

★ Bruschette

Coarse-textured Italian bread
Peeled garlic cloves
Extra-virgin olive oil

● Slice bread half-inch thick. Toast bread over grill until grill marks appear. Rub hot bread with peeled garlic. Drizzle with olive oil.

Speedy Shrimp Curry

★ **Cantaloupe Salad**
★ **Yogurt Dressing**
★ **Speedy Shrimp Curry**
★ **Walnut-Buttered Spinach**

Strained squash, sold in jars as baby food, makes an interesting sauce base for this shrimp curry for two. For a flavorful side dish, offer spinach with butter and toasted walnuts. A salad of cantaloupe cubes tossed with raisins, red onion rings and yogurt dressing would round out the meal nicely. All of the recipes are easily multiplied to feed four or more.

Curry is a good vehicle for leftovers. The same recipe could be made with cubes of cooked chicken or turkey, leftover roast lamb, beef, pork or even fish. Canned tuna or salmon would also work nicely. If you're feeling very extravagant, make a luxury version of the dish with chunks of lobster.

★ Speedy Shrimp Curry

1 tablespoon vegetable oil
1 medium onion, sliced
1 clove garlic, minced
½ cup diced sweet red pepper
½ pound medium shrimp,
*   peeled and deveined*
½ tart apple, peeled and chopped
1 tablespoon curry powder
½ cup chicken broth
1 jar (4½ ounces) strained squash baby food
Salt and pepper to taste
1½ cups cooked rice

• Heat oil in medium-size skillet. Saute onion, garlic and red pepper until pepper begins to soften. Add shrimp, apple and curry powder. Continue cooking, stirring frequently, for five minutes. Stir in chicken broth and strained squash. Cook over low heat until shrimp are cooked through and sauce is blended. Season to taste with salt and pepper. Serve over hot rice.

— *Makes two servings.*

★ Walnut-Buttered Spinach

1 pound fresh spinach
or 1 (10 ounce) box frozen leaf spinach
1 tablespoon butter
¼ cup walnut halves
Salt, pepper to taste

• Wash spinach to remove all traces of sand. Place in a large pot with water that remains on leaves from washing. Cover pot and steam about three minutes or until slightly wilted but still bright in color. (If frozen spinach is used, prepare according to package directions.)

• While spinach cooks, heat butter in small skillet and saute walnut halves. Drain cooked spinach, toss with walnut and butter mixture. Season to taste.

— *Makes two servings.*

★ Cantaloupe Salad

1 cup fresh cantaloupe cubes
2 tablespoons raisins
1 small red onion, peeled, sliced
Yogurt Dressing (see recipe)
Salad greens

• Arrange cantaloupe, raisins and onion slices on salad greens on two plates. Pass Yogurt Dressing.

— *Makes two servings.*

★ Yogurt Dressing

1 cup plain yogurt
3 tablespoons raspberry vinegar
2 tablespoons sugar
Salt, cayenne pepper to taste

• Mix ingredients. Use on Cantaloupe Salad or green salads.

— *Makes 1¼ cups.*

Meat

Broccoli with garlic mayonnaise and carrots
combined with coconut are the easy-to-make
side dishes for Curried Pork With Scallions.

Basic Hamburgers

★ **Raspberry-Cantaloupe Soup**
★ **Basic Hamburgers**
★ **Garlic Butter**
★ **Noodle Vegetable Stir-fry**

Raspberry-Cantaloupe Soup is a chunky fruit-and-yogurt soup that requires no cooking. Make it first, then put it in the freezer to chill while making the rest of the meal.

Noodle Vegetable Stir-fry normally would be made with fresh vegetables, but for anyone in a hurry, a good alternative is one of the frozen vegetable combinations available in plastic bags. The noodles were cooked according to package directions and then stir-fried with pine nuts, garlic and the vegetables to make an interesting and attractive starch-and-vegetable combination.

Serve the stir-fry with good old-fashioned hamburgers. A few tips could mean the difference between juicy, flavorful burgers and those that require effort to swallow. One secret of experienced burgermakers is to handle the meat lightly. Another is to brown the burgers without flattening them with a spatula. Some cooks season the meat mixture before cooking, but we prefer to cook the burgers unseasoned, then, at serving time, top with Garlic Butter.

★ Raspberry-Cantaloupe Soup

1 medium cantaloupe
1 container (6 ounces) raspberry
(or other fruit flavor) yogurt
2 tablespoons confectioners' sugar
Juice of one lime
Pinch of freshly grated nutmeg
Lime slices for garnish

• Cut cantaloupe in half, and discard seeds. Cut each half into eighths and remove rind with small knife or vegetable peeler. Place peeled wedges in food processor and process until melon is reduced to small pieces. Add yogurt, sugar, lime juice and nutmeg. Process for a second or two to blend flavors (mixture should remain chunky). Chill in freezer about 30 minutes. Serve in chilled bowls, hollowed melon halves or cups garnished with lime slice.

— *Makes four to six servings.*

★ Noodle Vegetable Stir-fry

8 ounces wide noodles
1 package (16 ounces) frozen
mixed vegetables
2 tablespoons vegetable oil
1 clove garlic, finely minced
1 tablespoon pine nuts
Salt, pepper

• Cook noodles according to package directions. While noodles cook, remove frozen vegetables from package, place in colander and immerse in hot water for a few seconds to thaw quickly. Drain thoroughly. Drain noodles and set aside.

• In wok or large skillet, heat oil to sizzling. Add garlic and pine nuts, and cook a second or two. (Do not brown garlic or it will turn bitter.) Add well-drained vegetables to skillet and stir-fry a minute or two. Add drained noodles and continue cooking, stirring constantly, about five minutes. Season to taste with salt and pepper.

— *Makes four to six servings.*

★ Basic Hamburgers

1½ pounds ground beef
1 teaspoon salt
¼ teaspoon pepper
Garlic Butter (see recipe)

• Shape meat lightly into six patties. Brown patties, uncovered, in large heavy skillet over moderately high heat. Do not press with spatula during cooking or you'll lose flavorful juices. Cooking should take about an additional four minutes per side for medium rare. At serving time, season with salt and pepper and place a little Garlic Butter on each one.

— *Makes six servings.*

★ Garlic Butter

4 tablespoons unsalted butter, softened
1 clove garlic, finely minced
Salt, white pepper

• With fork, blend butter with garlic and seasonings. Let stand, covered with plastic wrap, to blend flavors for at least 15 minutes.

— *Makes enough for six burgers.*

Quick Mix Chili

Avocado and Orange Salad
★ Quick Mix Chili
★ (Basic Chili Seasoning)
★ Corn and Pepper Corn Bread

Take the time to make a basic seasoning mix for chili, and the next few times you make chili, you have only to brown the beef and cook it briefly with some of your already-made seasoning.

The recipe is generously spiced and deliciously different. The heat of the chili powder you buy will determine how much of the spice needs to be added. Our quantity — five tablespoons — should be adequate for a medium-hot chili. The modest amount of unsweetened chocolate will thicken the sauce and make it richer. Try it.

With the chili, serve a cooling salad of avocado slices and orange sections with French dressing. As a hearty accompaniment, cook up a batch of corn bread using a box of mix, some corn kernels (for flavor and texture) and some hot pepper. It will take just a few minutes and add immeasurably to the enjoyment of the chili.

★ Basic Chili Seasoning

5 tablespoons oil
5 tablespoons chili powder
2 tablespoons toasted sesame seeds (see note)
½ cup well-drained tomatoes
1 tablespoon tomato paste
¼ ounce unsweetened chocolate

• Heat oil in heavy skillet. Stir in chili powder. Cook over medium heat for about five minutes. In blender or processor, blend sesame seeds, tomatoes, tomato paste and chocolate to make a smooth mixture. Add sesame mixture to mixture in skillet. Cook over medium heat for 10 minutes to blend flavors. Use as directed in Quick Mix Chili recipe. Refrigerate or freeze unused seasoning mix.

• Note: To toast sesame seeds, place in a heavy skillet and cook over medium heat until seeds are golden. Shake pan constantly during cooking to prevent scorching.

— *Makes enough for three pounds of ground beef.*

★ Quick Mix Chili

1 pound lean ground beef
1 medium onion, chopped
1 clove garlic, minced
¼ cup Basic Chili Seasoning (see recipe)
Salt, pepper to taste
2 cans kidney beans, drained, rinsed
1 chopped raw onion

• Combine ground beef, onion and garlic in a large skillet, and saute until meat is browned and onion soft. Remove and discard any excess fat. Stir in chili seasoning mix, and season to taste with salt and pepper. Simmer about 15 minutes to blend flavors. Stir in well-drained beans, and cook an additional 15 minutes over low heat. Serve with chopped onion.

— *Makes six servings.*

★ Corn and Pepper Corn Bread

1 package (8½ ounces) corn muffin mix
1 egg
⅓ cup milk
1 cup corn kernels, cooked and drained
1 teaspoon chopped parsley
¼ teaspoon dried red pepper flakes
2 tablespoons grated Parmesan cheese

• Blend ingredients in a mixing bowl. Pour into a greased eight-inch-square baking pan, and bake about 25 minutes.

— *Makes six servings.*

Oriental Beef Stir-fry

★ **Egg Drop Soup**
★ **Oriental Beef Stir-fry**
  Rice

Oriental stir-fry dishes are attractive to American cooks for a variety of reasons, not the least of which is that they stretch modest amounts of costly meats or seafood. The meat, rice and vegetable combinations are also ideal for those times when you must prepare a meal in minutes.

Oriental Beef Stir-fry makes a pound and a half of sirloin steak feed six diners well. If you want to keep the meal in an Asian mood, start with light and delicious Egg Drop Soup made with good-quality canned (or fresh) chicken broth to which you have added eggs and green onion for flavor, substance and color.

★ Oriental Beef Stir-fry

1½ pounds sirloin,
  cut into very thin strips
¼ cup peanut or vegetable oil
1 clove garlic, minced
1 cup thinly sliced carrots
2 stalks celery, diagonally sliced
1 large green pepper,
  cut into ¾-inch squares
1 zucchini, thinly sliced
¼ pound mushrooms, sliced
1 cup chicken broth
¼ cup soy sauce
1½ tablespoons cornstarch
3 cups hot cooked rice

• Brown steak strips in hot oil in large skillet or wok. Push to the side and add garlic and vegetables. Stir-fry about three minutes.

• Combine broth, soy sauce and cornstarch. Add to skillet and cook until clear and thickened. Serve over fluffy rice.

— *Makes six servings.*

94

★ Egg Drop Soup

7 cups chicken broth, fat removed
3 tablespoons cornstarch
¼ cup water
½ teaspoon sugar
1 teaspoon salt
2 eggs, beaten
1 teaspoon slivered fresh ginger
¼ cup chopped green onions

● Heat broth to boiling. Make paste of cornstarch and one-quarter cup water. Stir cornstarch into hot broth with sugar and salt. Return broth to boil, stirring constantly. Mixture should thicken slightly.

● Reduce heat. Add eggs gradually, beating well to separate into shreds.

● Remove from heat; add ginger and onions. Serve at once.

— *Makes six servings.*

TIPS/*STIR-FRYING AND MORE*

● **Cut ingredients** for stir-frying into fairly small pieces. The idea is to cook everything quickly in the smallest amount of oil.

● Although stir-fry ingredients should be cut into small pieces, the finished dish will be more interesting if there is **some variety** in the shapes. Cut stalks on the diagonal, for example, and hollow vegetables like peppers in rings or squares.

● **Move pieces of food quickly** from the well of the wok, where the oil collects, to the sloping sides, where excess oil can drain into the well.

● When using **cornstarch** to thicken a sauce, gradually stir some of the liquid to be thickened into the cornstarch to dissolve and thin it. Then add the thinned cornstarch to the rest of the liquid.

Pressure Cooker Beef Stew

> ★ **Carrot, Grape and Walnut Salad**
> ★ **Pressure Cooker Beef Stew**
>   **Buttered Noodles**

I f you own and use a pressure cooker, one of the temptations is to cook everything — meat and vegetables — in the cooker at one time. Yet if you time the pressure cooking to make the meat tender, you've probably done in the vegetables.

This recipe is a solution if you like the blended flavors of a stew with a bit of texture to the vegetables. In Pressure Cooker Beef Stew, the crisp-tender vegetables are cooked separately while the pressure cooker tender-cooks the beef in a sauce flavored with soy, ginger, garlic and sherry. At the last minute, both are combined and heated in the sauce formed with the beef. The stew is delicious over buttered noodles.

For a colorful salad, we've combined grated carrots, small green grapes and walnuts with a sweetened mustard vinaigrette.

★ Pressure Cooker Beef Stew

*1½ pounds lean beef chuck,
   cut into ¾-inch cubes
3 tablespoons oil, divided
½ cup chicken broth
1 clove garlic, minced
1 teaspoon minced ginger
2 tablespoons soy sauce
1 tablespoon dry sherry
½ teaspoon sugar
1 large onion, sliced
2 ribs celery, sliced diagonally
1 large green pepper, cut into strips
½ pound mushrooms, caps only*

• Dry beef cubes thoroughly with paper towels. Heat two tablespoons oil in pressure cooker and brown beef in oil. Add broth, garlic, ginger, soy, sherry and sugar. Cover pressure cooker. Set control at 10 and place over high heat until control jiggles. Reduce heat and cook six minutes. Run cold water over the cooker to reduce pressure instantly.

• While beef cooks, heat remaining oil in large skillet or wok. Stir-fry sliced onion, celery, green pepper and mushroom caps about two minutes. Vegetables should be quite crisp.
• Spoon beef and sauce into vegetables and heat about five minutes or until flavors blend. Serve over buttered noodles.
— *Makes four to five servings.*

★ Carrot, Grape and Walnut Salad

4 large carrots, grated
2 cups small green seedless grapes
¼ cup walnut halves
3 tablespoons oil
1 tablespoon sherry vinegar
1 teaspoon Dijon-type mustard
1 teaspoon sugar
¼ teaspoon salt

• Combine carrots, seedless grapes and walnut halves. Blend oil, vinegar, mustard, sugar and salt well. Add to carrot mixture and stir to blend well.
— *Makes four to five servings.*

Veal Elaine

Avocado and Grapefruit Salad
★ Smoky Lentil Soup
★ Veal Elaine
Mashed Potatoes
Kale

The temperature is unspeakably low and you're thinking of hearty foods. Now's the time for a dinner that has the extra oomph of a cup of substantial soup.

On a frigid Sunday, the soup was hearty lentil, given a nice smoky flavor with two pieces of inexpensive smoked pork neck bones. The entree was thin veal chops with mushrooms. Mashed potatoes and kale were the stick-to-your-ribs vegetable accompaniments; salad with Vitamin C to spare was made with fresh grapefruit, avocado, romaine and a homemade vinaigrette dressing.

Although the food was substantial, the menu was surprisingly easy. Early in the day, I started to marinate the veal chops. The soup cooked in an hour and a half but it reheats beautifully so you can make it whenever you have time, then put it back on the heat just before the meal.

★ Veal Elaine

4 thin veal chops
¼ cup oil
1 teaspoon white wine vinegar
½ teaspoon thyme
2 large cloves garlic, minced
1 tablespoon butter
6 large mushrooms, sliced
Salt, pepper

• Place chops in a single layer in a glass baking dish. Mix oil, vinegar, thyme and garlic, and pour over chops. Cover with plastic wrap and marinate in the refrigerator for several hours.

• At cooking time, wipe chops dry with paper towels. Melt butter and brown chops on both sides in melted butter. Now add mushrooms to pan. Lift chops so mushrooms cook under chops. When mushrooms are soft and chops cooked through, serve with pan juices.

— *Makes four servings.*

★ Smoky Lentil Soup

½ pound lentils
1 carrot, pared, sliced
1 large onion, peeled, chopped
1 large stalk celery, chopped
2 small pieces smoked pork bones
  or ham hocks
4 sprigs parsley, chopped
1½ quarts water
Salt, pepper

• Place lentils, vegetables, pork bones or ham hocks, parsley and water in heavy pot. Bring to boil, then reduce heat to simmer. Skim to remove surface accumulation as it forms. Cook, uncovered, until lentils are tender. (Smoked pork bones have very little meat but provide a great deal of flavor. They can be discarded at the end of cooking time.) If soup is too thick, add water. Season to taste with salt and pepper.

— *Makes four to six servings.*

TIPS/*MASHED POTATOES*

• **Mashed potatoes** went out of fashion when Americans grew weary of the sorry instant mashed potatoes that were served everywhere in the name of convenience. The good news is that real mashed potatoes are back on the table everywhere from diners to fancy restaurants.

• One of the easiest versions of mashed potatoes is made with unpeeled **red bliss potatoes**. The skins give more flavor and texture to the dish.

• Some cooks use milk as **the liquid** in mashed potatoes and some even add cream. Our favorite mashed potatoes contain a mixture of half milk and half water that was used to cook the potatoes.

• **Herbs and spices** — even minced onions sauteed in butter — can perk up the flavor of mashed potatoes. Grated Parmesan cheese makes them creamier and richer.

Veal With Anchovy Crumbs

★ **Veal With Anchovy Crumbs**
★ **Spinach Noodles**
    With Black Olives and Pine Nuts
★ **Corn With Sauteed Onions**

A reasonably well-organized cook can put this appealing meal together in less than 30 minutes. Veal With Anchovy Crumbs starts with paper-thin veal slices that brown in just a few seconds per side. Spinach Noodles With Black Olives and Pine Nuts will take less than 20 minutes. Corn With Sauteed Onions is the colorful vegetable, which can be made with fresh corn in season or good frozen corn.

★ Veal With Anchovy Crumbs

1 pound veal scallops
3 tablespoons butter, divided
10 low-salt shredded-wheat crackers
2 anchovy filets
Freshly ground pepper
Lemon wedges and parsley for garnish

• Pound individual veal scallops until thin between two sheets of plastic wrap. Heat two tablespoons of the butter in a large skillet. Brown the veal pieces on both sides in the butter. Remove to warm plate.

• Process or crumble crackers. Melt remaining butter in skillet. Stir in anchovy filets, mashing with fork to blend into butter. Add crumbs and cook, over medium heat, to brown crumbs and absorb butter. Season reserved veal with fresh pepper, and sprinkle with anchovy crumbs. Serve garnished with lemon wedges and parsley.

— *Makes four servings.*

★ Corn With Sauteed Onions

2 tablespoons butter
1 small onion, peeled and sliced
2 cups corn kernels
Salt, white pepper

• Heat butter in skillet. Saute onion in butter until softened and beginning to brown. Add corn, cooking for a minute or two. Season to taste with salt and white pepper.

— *Makes four servings.*

★ Spinach Noodles With Black Olives and Pine Nuts

8 ounces spinach noodles
12 cured black olives
3 tablespoons olive oil
1 clove garlic, minced
1 tablespoon pine nuts
2 tablespoons chopped Italian parsley
Salt, hot red pepper flakes to taste

• Cook noodles according to package directions. While noodles cook, remove pits from black olives and chop olives coarsely. Heat olive oil. Add garlic and saute one minute. Add olives, pine nuts and continue cooking until pine nuts begin to brown. Stir in parsley, salt and pepper flakes.

• Drain cooked noodles and toss with olive mixture.

— *Makes four side-dish servings.*

Peppered Lamb Chops

★ **Peppered Lamb Chops**
★ **Sweet Pepper Scramble**
Orange-Cinnamon Couscous

W ith the availability of fresh hot peppers like Mexico's jalapenos and dried varieties like China's Szechwan peppercorns, contemporary cooks can now concoct all manner of international sizzlers.

But even if you don't have a pantry packed with exotic peppers, it's possible to prepare a dish that's sure to please fire-eaters.

Peppered Lamb Chops are made with ordinary black peppercorns that you crush roughly and use to coat tiny lamb chops before sauteing them in butter. The flavor of the lamb, like that of beef, is assertive enough to balance the pepper bite.

With the lamb, serve another pepper dish, this one a sweet, not hot, mixture that includes Italian frying peppers and regular green and red peppers. If you're feeling extravagant, and if they're available at your market, add some strips of more expensive yellow peppers.

An interesting and rather Moroccan side dish with the lamb and peppers would be freshly cooked couscous to which you've added butter, a grating of fresh orange zest and a hint of cinnamon.

★ Peppered Lamb Chops

1 tablespoon whole black peppercorns
4 loin lamb chops
2 tablespoons butter, divided
2 shallots, finely minced
2 tablespoons gin

• On the kitchen counter or a solid cutting block, place peppercorns in a single layer on a sheet of plastic wrap. Cover with second sheet of plastic wrap. With bottom of heavy skillet or pot, crush peppercorns coarsely. Remove top layer of plastic wrap. Press lamb chops into crushed peppercorns to coat lightly.

• In a heavy skillet large enough to hold chops in a single layer, melt one tablespoon of butter. When butter begins to sizzle, place chops in pan, and brown on both sides over medium to high heat. Continue to cook until chops are very rare. Remove chops from pan to a warmed platter (they will continue to cook to rare) while making sauce.

• To juices in pan, add chopped shallots. Saute about a minute to cook shallots. Pour gin into pan and flame immediately, stirring with long-handled spoon to dissolve browned particles in pan. Stir in remaining butter and, when butter melts and is incorporated into pan juices, pour over lamb chops and serve.

— *Makes two servings.*

★ Sweet Pepper Scramble

Firm sweet peppers, mix colors and types
2 tablespoons oil
Salt, pepper to taste

• Wash, seed and slice peppers into rings. (Use two sweet bell peppers and two Italian frying peppers.) Heat oil in large skillet. Saute peppers until tender but slightly firm. Season to taste.

— *Makes two servings.*

TIPS/*COUSCOUS AND MORE*

• **Instant couscous** is a fast-cooking starch and although it is not as light and fluffy as the authentic version served in Morocco, it is nonetheless delicious and versatile. To make it, heat butter and broth to boiling, then add the grain. (See package for amounts and times). When grain has absorbed the butter and liquid, add desired seasonings.

• To remove the seeds from **green peppers** easily, slice off the stem end of each pepper and run a paring knife around the inside, separating seed membrane from pepper walls. Pull out membrane and seeds.

• For **a palate cooler** after a pepper-heated dish, offer cucumber slices with yogurt, chopped fresh mint and scallions.

Lamb Steak With Beans and Mint Beurre Blanc

★Sesame-Soy Carrot Salad
★ Lamb Steak With Beans
  and Mint Beurre Blanc
★ Quick Potato Cake

L amb for two? It doesn't always mean lamb chops. A lamb steak, cut from the leg, is a delicious alternative, and unless you're a big meat eater, a single steak weighing a pound or less should serve both of you.

Lamb steak has a higher percentage of lean meat to fat and bone than do the more expensive chops. And it's quick and easy to prepare, just right for cooks in a hurry.

If you're a traditionalist, you'll probably serve the lamb with a dab of mint jelly. If you're more adventurous, you'll try our Mint Beurre Blanc Sauce.

Keep the rest of the meal simple and hearty with fresh wax beans, steamed and served with a little of the Mint Beurre Blanc and a Quick Potato Cake made with frozen unpeeled french fries sauteed, then held together with a beaten egg. For salad, offer grated carrots tossed with a sesame-soy dressing. If you own a food processor, let it grate the carrots for you.

★ Lamb Steak With Beans and Mint Beurre Blanc

---

1 lamb steak (1 pound or less)
3 tablespoons chopped shallots
⅓ cup dry vermouth
¼ cup mint vinegar
¼ pound (1 stick) chilled unsalted butter
Salt and white pepper
Few drops mint vinegar
½ pound wax beans, steamed

• With a sharp knife, make small cuts several inches apart around the outer edge of the steak to prevent curling while cooking. In a nonstick skillet, over high heat, brown steak on both sides. Reduce heat and continue cooking five to 10 minutes or until desired doneness is reached. Serve with steamed wax beans and Mint Beurre Blanc.

• To make Mint Beurre Blanc, place chopped shallots, vermouth and mint vinegar in a heavy pan and cook, over medium heat, until liquid is reduced to about two tablespoons.

• Remove pan from heat. Strain out chopped shallots. Return liquid to pan. Whisk in butter a tablespoon at a time. Continue whisking for a few seconds after all butter is incorporated. Sauce should be light and frothy. Season with salt, pepper and a few drops of vinegar. Serve warm over cooked lamb and wax beans. Leftover Beurre Blanc can be refrigerated and used as mint butter over vegetables, poultry or meat.

— *Makes two servings.*

★ Quick Potato Cake

20 pieces frozen french fries
1 tablespoon oil
1 egg, beaten lightly
Salt and pepper

• Brown the frozen french fries on both sides in the oil in a small, hot skillet. Reduce heat; stir in beaten egg. Season with salt and pepper. Cover and cook over low heat until egg sets. Flip cooked potato cake onto serving plate. Cut in half and serve.

— *Makes two servings.*

★ Sesame-Soy Carrot Salad

6 medium carrots
Salt
1 tablespoon light soy sauce
1 tablespoon sesame oil
1 teaspoon sugar
Chopped scallions (optional)

• Grate carrots with grater or food processor. Place in colander. Sprinkle with salt and let stand for 15 minutes. Measure soy sauce, sesame oil and sugar into a cup. Blend thoroughly. Rinse carrots and drain. Add dressing and toss to blend thoroughly. Sprinkle with chopped scallions, if desired.

— *Makes four servings.*

Stir-fry Green Beans With Pork

★ **American Chicken Velvet Corn Soup**
★ **Stir-fry Green Beans With Pork**
Rice

Our version of Chinese chicken corn soup uses whole kernels, cut fresh from the cob, rather than canned cream corn, which most Chinese restaurants use. Although the soup is rich and filling, it's made without butter or cream and is remarkably low in calories.

Since there's chicken in the soup, we've included a main dish that's light on meat: Stir-fry Green Beans with Pork. Rice would make an ideal accompaniment for these two Chinese restaurant favorites.

★ Stir-fry Green Beans With Pork

1 pound green beans
¼ pound lean pork
¼ cup oil, divided
3 slices ginger, peeled, minced
1 clove garlic, minced
1 tablespoon sugar
1 tablespoon soy sauce
1 tablespoon water
1 teaspoon sesame oil

• Remove stems from beans and put beans in enough boiling salted water to cover. Cook just until crisp-tender, about two minutes. Drain in a colander under cold running water.

• Finely mince the pork. Brown in two tablespoons oil with ginger and garlic. Add sugar, soy and water, and stir to blend well.

• In remaining oil, stir-fry drained green beans over high heat until beans begin to sizzle. Add meat sauce and continue cooking two more minutes. Serve at room temperature, sprinkled with sesame oil.

— *Makes four to six servings.*

★ American Chicken Velvet Corn Soup

¼ pound ground chicken (or turkey)
3 egg whites, divided
4 ears white or yellow corn
4 cups chicken stock
2 tablespoons cornstarch dissolved in water
Salt to taste
3 scallions, chopped
Few drops Oriental sesame oil

• Combine ground chicken with one egg white and the kernels cut from the ears of corn. Beat remaining egg whites separately and set aside.

• Bring chicken broth to a boil. Add chicken and corn mixture. Cook two minutes. Add dissolved cornstarch, stirring until soup is thickened.

• Reduce heat. Add beaten egg whites slowly. Stir until well-blended. Add salt if necessary. Pour into serving bowl. Sprinkle with chopped scallions and sesame oil.

— *Makes four to six servings.*

TIPS/*SESAME OIL AND MORE*

• **Sesame oil**, which is used in Asian cooking as a seasoning, has a very pronounced flavoring and should be used sparingly.

• In **stir-frying**, heat the wok before adding oil. This helps to keep the oil from breaking down.

• To **remove corn from the cob** without making a mess, use an angel cake pan. Wedge the narrow end of the ear into the tube of the pan. Using a sharp knife, slice off the kernels so that they fall into the pan.

Calico Pork

```
★ Calico Pork
★ Crusty Fried Potatoes
★ Tomatoes With Basil Mayonnaise
  Corn
```

Named for the bright color that sweet red pepper rings give to this attractive dish, Calico Pork is a happy combination of garlic-seasoned pork strips, sauteed sweet peppers, cabbage and onion. Cumin and as much hot red pepper as your taste dictates give the recipe exciting flavor.

Accompaniments? Steamed rice would be acceptable, and it's the easiest choice, but we like the texture and flavor balance provided by Crusty Fried Potatoes made with pre-cooked potatoes. Some fresh corn would also help to fill the plate nicely.

For a salad, thick slices of tomato would be delicious as is or with a dollop of Basil Mayonnaise.

★ Calico Pork

1 pork steak, about one pound
2 small cloves garlic, minced
Salt, pepper
Salad oil
2 medium sweet red peppers,
  sliced thinly into rings
½ cup chopped onion
3 cups coarsely chopped cabbage
1 teaspoon cumin
1 or 2 small dried hot red peppers (to taste)
2 or 3 tablespoons water or chicken stock

• Cut pork steak into strips about one-half inch wide and one inch long. In a large nonstick skillet over high heat, saute strips with garlic until pork is browned on all surfaces, about five minutes. Season lightly with salt and pepper. If necessary, add a few drops of oil to keep meat from sticking.

• Remove pork and garlic from skillet and set aside. Reduce heat to medium. Add one teaspoon of oil to pan. In hot oil, stir-fry pepper rings about five minutes or until they begin to soften. Add onion and cook, stirring, for an additional five minutes. Stir in cabbage, cumin and hot red pepper to taste. Continue cooking, stirring constantly, for five minutes. Return pork cubes to mixture, cover and cook until pork is tender and cooked through. If mixture seems too dry, stir in a few tablespoons of water or chicken stock.

— *Makes four servings.*

★ Crusty Fried Potatoes

4 large potatoes, cooked, thickly sliced
2 tablespoons olive oil
Salt and pepper to taste
Chopped parsley (optional)

• In large skillet, saute potatoes in hot oil, turning potatoes during cooking with a spatula, until they are crusty and evenly browned. Sprinkle with salt and pepper and chopped parsley.

— *Makes four to six servings.*

★ Basil Mayonnaise

1 cup homemade mayonnaise
8 large basil leaves, cut in fine shreds
Freshly ground pepper

• Stir shredded basil leaves into mayonnaise. Season generously with pepper. Flavor improves with standing.

— *Makes one cup.*

Curried Pork With Scallions

★ **Curried Pork With Scallions**
  Rice
★ **Coconut Carrots**
  Cold Broccoli
    With Garlic Mayonnaise

Because curry loves coconut and rice, offer both with this good pork dish. Plain boiled rice will make a good blotter for the surplus sauce. Toast the coconut and add it, with butter, to steamed carrots for the delicious vegetable accompaniment.

Create a compatible salad by combining cooked cold broccoli with garlic mayonnaise.

★ Curried Pork With Scallions

1 pound thinly sliced, boneless pork cutlets
Curry powder
Salt, pepper to taste
3 tablespoons butter, divided
1 bunch scallions, trimmed, chopped

• In a skillet, season pork pieces on both sides with curry, salt and pepper. Sprinkle lightly for mild curry flavor, more heavily for a more spicy dish.

• Heat two tablespoons of the butter in the skillet. Brown pork pieces without crowding. (You may have to remove some pieces as they brown to make room for others.) When all pork pieces are browned, return to pan with remaining butter and scallions. Cook, stirring to blend scallions and juices, for about three minutes. Cover, reduce heat to low, and let dish cook for 10 more minutes. Serve over fluffy rice.

— *Makes four to six servings.*

★ Coconut Carrots

2 cups thinly sliced carrots
1 tablespoon butter
⅓ cup toasted coconut
Salt, pepper

• Steam carrots until just tender. Toss with butter, toasted coconut and salt and pepper to taste. To toast coconut, pour sweetened flake coconut into heavy, ungreased skillet over medium heat and toast, shaking the pan constantly, until nicely browned.

— *Makes four servings.*

TIPS/*CURRY*

• Commercial **curry powder** was developed as a convenience, but in India, where curries originated, spices are blended in varying proportions for individual dishes. The most commonly used spices in Indian curries are cardamom, cayenne pepper, coriander, cumin, cloves, ginger, fenugreek, turmeric, mace and black pepper.

• **Freshly ground spices** give a curry blend the liveliest flavor. To grind your own quicky and easily, invest in a small electric coffee mill. Clean the mill thoroughly after each use. Since ground spices lose flavor quickly, you'll want to grind just enough for a few days' use.

• **Fenugreek**, one of the ingredients in many curry powder blends, is a pulse used as a spice. (A pulse is the seed of a plant that bears pods.) The very aromatic seeds are so small that it takes some 2,500 of them to make an ounce.

• **Nutmeg and mace** come from the nutmeg tree. Nutmeg is the seed of the tree. Mace is the netlike wrapping of the nutmeg seed. Both are pungent and should be used sparingly in curry blends.

Pork Chops With Cumin Rice

Pork Chops With Cumin Rice is an oven-cooked dish, so for energy efficiency it would be wise to cook as much as possible of the rest of the meal in the oven at the same time. Corn custard, made with canned corn, assembles in seconds, bakes in 35 to 45 minutes.

Crisp slaw made with freshly chopped cabbage and well-seasoned mayonnaise dressing would round out the meal nicely.

★ Pork Chops With Cumin Rice

5 or 6 pork chops about ½-inch thick
Salt and pepper
1 tablespoon vegetable oil
3 tablespoons each chopped onion
   and green pepper
1 cup uncooked rice
2 cups boiling chicken broth
1 teaspoon Worcestershire sauce
½ teaspoon each salt and cumin seed

• Season chops with salt and pepper and brown on each side in oil. Remove chops. Drain off excess fat and discard. Add remaining ingredients to pan, stirring to loosen brown particles. Cover and bake at 350 degrees for 20 minutes. Add chops and continue cooking for 10 minutes or until meat and rice are tender and liquid is absorbed. Fluff rice with a fork.

— Makes four to six servings.

★ Corn Custard

1 (pound) can whole kernel corn, drained
3 eggs, beaten
4 cups milk
1½ teaspoons salt

112

• Combine ingredients in greased 1½-quart casserole. Bake at 350 for 35 to 45 minutes.

— *Makes six servings.*

TIPS/*SEASONINGS*

• **Worcestershire sauce** is a soy-sauce-based condiment of English origin. It is heavily seasoned and contains extracts of vegetables — primarily carrots and onions. In an emergency, substitute plain soy sauce, preferably the dark type.

• **Cumin** is an aromatic spice used in many curry powders and in chili powders. Cumin seed will release its flavor and fragrance more fully if crushed slightly before it is added to a recipe.

• Because chopping **onion** is a smelly, messy chore, many cooks chop several onions at a time, storing the surplus for subsequent uses. The chopped onions, placed in a colander then rinsed with cold water and well-drained, lose their eye-stinging component, which is water soluble. Rinsing also keeps the onions from darkening during storage.

• For oomph, add a seeded finely chopped **Jalapeno pepper** to corn pudding before baking.

Quick Pork and Apple Kraut

Spinach and Orange Salad
★ Quick Pork and Apple Kraut
Mashed Potatoes

Quick Pork and Apple Kraut, made with thinly sliced pork tenderloin, cooks to delicious doneness in a little more than a half-hour. To minimize saltiness, the sauerkraut for the recipe is well rinsed before cooking. Slices of tart apple (Granny Smith would be a good choice) give the dish interesting flavor and texture.

To round out the menu and add a little welcome color, include a salad of fresh spinach, red onion rings and orange slices tossed with a little herb vinaigrette. Old-fashioned mashed potatoes would make an appropriate foil for the kraut.

★ Quick Pork and Apple Kraut

1 pound thinly sliced pork tenderloin
3 tablespoons butter, divided
2 tart apples, pared, thinly sliced
1 pound sauerkraut
⅔ cup dry white wine
2 tablespoons brown sugar
Salt, white pepper to taste

• In a large skillet, brown pork slices in two tablespoons butter. When both sides are browned, add apple slices. Saute five minutes, stirring occasionally to cook apples evenly.

• Rinse sauerkraut well by running cold water over it in a colander. Drain well. Add drained kraut to skillet, stirring to blend. Stir in white wine. Simmer, covered, for 10 minutes.

• Remove cover, stir in brown sugar and remaining butter. Taste and add salt if necessary (will depend on saltiness of kraut) and pepper. Simmer, uncovered, five minutes longer.

— *Makes four to five servings.*

Italian Bacon-Cabbage Soup

Spinach Salad
★ Italian Bacon-Cabbage Soup
Crusty Bread

Winter soup, hot, hearty and so filled with ingredients that it can make a meal, sounds like an all-day project to make. But in northern Italy, where the mountain air makes appetites sharp, there's a soup that satisfies yet takes little more than half an hour to make.

Cabbage, rice and bacon give the soup its heft. Some onions, sauteed in butter, add mellow overtones. Crusty country bread and a spinach salad would round out the meal nicely.

★ Italian Bacon-Cabbage Soup

1 tablespoon butter
1 tablespoon olive oil
1 cup chopped onion
1 medium-size head of cabbage, shredded
4 thick slices bacon
8 cups beef stock
¾ cup rice
2 tablespoons parsley
Salt and pepper to taste
½ cup freshly grated Parmesan cheese

• Melt the butter with olive oil in a pan with a large bottom surface and high sides. Add onion, and fry until it softens. Add cabbage, and fry for five minutes until cabbage is well-coated with butter and begins to soften.

• While cabbage cooks, saute bacon in a small skillet, until the bacon has released much of its fat but is not browned. Remove bacon from skillet and drain on paper towels.

• Chop bacon into large squares. Add to cabbage with beef stock. Bring to boil, then reduce heat and simmer for 15 minutes. Stir in rice. Return heat to high, and when soup begins to boil, reduce to simmer. Cook, stirring occasionally, for 15 minutes longer. Stir in parsley. Add salt and pepper to taste. Spoon into bowls, and sprinkle with grated Parmesan.

— *Makes four generous servings.*

Italian Sausage Pie

Crudites
★ Italian Sausage Pie

D id you know you can bake a sausage pie quicker than a cat can wink its eye? The trick is to top a delicious sausage filling with one of the new ready-to-bake pastry rounds.

The pastry rounds are now available, two to a box, in the refrigerated-dough department of many supermarkets. You can slip one, just as it comes from the box, on top of the sausage filling, or you can be creative, trimming the pastry with cutouts that you've made from the second pastry round.

We used a dove-shaped cookie cutter for one of the designs on the pastry. Look around. You'll find lots of ideas in your kitchen and in the stores that sell unusual kitchen tools.

We like this handsome yet hearty dish as the main attraction in a meal that begins with raw vegetable crudites.

★ Italian Sausage Pie

2 9-inch pastry rounds
1 pound sweet Italian sausage
½ pound mushrooms, halved
1 large green pepper, sliced
1 large sweet red pepper, sliced
1 large onion, sliced
¼ cup minced parsley
1 tablespoon flour
1 tablespoon butter
1 cup beef consomme
Salt, pepper to taste
Egg yolk beaten with one tablespoon water

• Remove pouch of pastry from box and let stand at room temperature while preparing filling. Place sausage in a large skillet and cover with water. Cook just long enough to firm sausage (about five minutes). Remove sausage and drain, removing casing. Cut into one-inch segments.

• Wipe skillet dry, and in it saute sausage with mushrooms, peppers, onion and parsley for 20 minutes or until sausage is cooked through and vegetables are soft. Remove any excess fat, if necessary.

- Blend flour and butter. Add butter-flour and consomme to sausage and cook, stirring, until thickened. Season to taste with salt and pepper.
- Sprinkle pastry rounds lightly with flour and spread flour evenly over entire surface. Use second round to make pastry cutouts. (Any leftover pastry can be cut out, sprinkled with seasoned salt or herbs and baked on a cookie sheet for snacks.) Brush cutouts with egg-water mixture, and position on circle of pastry. When cutouts are arranged, brush entire surface with egg wash. Cut slashes into pastry for steam to escape.
- Place hot filling in 9-inch pie plate. Top with decorated pastry. Crimp edges of pastry to seal to edge of plate. Bake at 450 degrees for 9 to 11 minutes or until browned.

— *Makes six servings.*

TIPS/*SAUSAGE*

- Basic **Italian sweet sausage** is flavored with fennel seeds. A hot version has crushed red pepper and coarse black pepper.

- **Luganega**, a sausage from Northeast Italy, contains grated Parmesan cheese, wine, garlic and oregano.

- **German Bockwurst**, a blend of veal and pork, features the subtle flavors of parsley and chives and is delicious grilled and served with spicy mustard.

- **Spanish chorizo sausage** is a basic ingredient in many of the dishes in that country. Paprika gives the pork-based chorizo an orangish color and deep flavor.

- Delicate **boudins blancs** from France are chicken-based white sausages. The small link sausages are delicious grilled or pan-fried.

- **Merguez**, lamb sausages said to have originated in Tunisia, are highly spiced and excellent for outdoor grilling.

Spicy Sausage Bites

W hat do you do when you have little money and only minutes to prepare party food? You could serve chips or crudites and a dip, crackers and cheese, or a dozen other cliches. Or you could dazzle your guests with Spicy Sausage Bites, Garlic Olives and Chinese Chicken Wings, all of which take more time to describe than they do to fix.

Use the sausage you like best. Sweet or hot Italian pork sausage would do nicely. So would Spanish chorizo or Moroccan lamb sausage. When it's cooked and cooled, peel off and discard the casings if they're tough. When ready to fill the pastries, cut up the sausage and set aside for filling.

★ Spicy Sausage Bites

2 pounds spicy sausage, cooked and cooled
1 package (1 pound) frozen phyllo, thawed
½ pound (2 sticks) butter, melted

• Remove sausage casings if tough. Chop sausage coarsely. Set aside.

• Unwrap the phyllo sheets. Without separating the individual sheets (there will be about 20 sheets in the package), cut through the stack to make rectangular strips, each strip about 4 by 10 inches.

• With the exception of the piece you are filling, cover all the phyllo dough with a damp cloth to keep this very thin dough from drying out.

• Work quickly with exposed phyllo. Remove the top strip of phyllo from the stack to a cutting board or washable work surface. Brush generously with melted butter, using a pastry brush.

• Bring the short side of the buttered phyllo strip to meet the long side, forming a triangular pocket. Place a heaping teaspoon of the chopped sausage in the pocket.

• Fold the pocket, along the triangle's base, toward the buttered surface. Continue folding to make new triangles until the entire phyllo strip has been used. The result will be a triangle-shape packet. Place the phyllo packet, seam side down, on an ungreased cookie sheet. Repeat with remaining dough and sausage slices.

• Bake at 400 degrees for five to seven minutes, or until dough is nicely browned and crisp. Unbaked packets can be frozen and baked as needed.

— *Makes 100 appetizers.*

★ Easy Garlic Olives

2 cups green or black olives
1 clove garlic
Good-quality olive oil to cover

• Drain liquid from olives if canned or bottled olives are used. Place olives in a jar with a cover and add bruised, fresh garlic clove. Cover with olive oil. Let stand, covered, at least 24 hours before serving to develop flavor. Garlic oil may be used for salad dressing.

— Makes one pint.

★ Chinese Chicken Wings

2 pounds chicken wings
2 tablespoons peanut oil
2 teaspoons shredded ginger
1 tablespoon grated lemon rind
1 tablespoon soy sauce
⅓ cup lemon juice
1 cup water
1 tablespoon sugar
1 teaspoon sesame oil

• Remove tips from chicken wings and reserve for stock-making. Separate wings at the joint to make two pieces. Heat peanut oil in large skillet or wok. Brown chicken wings in heated oil.

• Combine ginger, lemon rind, soy sauce, lemon juice, water, sugar and sesame oil. Add to pan with chicken wings and simmer until wings are tender, about 15 minutes. Remove wings from liquid and broil a minute or two to crisp skin.

— Makes six appetizer servings.

Pork Chops With Sage

★ **Pork Chops With Sage**
★ **Parsley Potatoes**
   Applesauce

Sometimes it takes just a few seasonings to make a hurried meal into a special one. Want an example? Saute some onion in oil before you brown pork chops in the pan with the onion. Crumble some sage leaves over the browned chops, pour in some white wine, season with salt and pepper and cover. The meat will cook to delicious doneness in just a few minutes.

While the chops cook, peel and cube some potatoes and cook until firm but tender. Drain the cooked potatoes, toss with butter and chopped parsley, salt and pepper at serving time.

For a quick side dish, heat applesauce and season with cinnamon.

★ Pork Chops With Sage

4 large pork chops
1 tablespoon oil
1 large onion, sliced
1 teaspoon dried sage leaves
½ cup dry white wine or vermouth
Salt, pepper

• Wipe chops dry for better browning. In oil, saute onion until soft. Add chops and brown on both sides. When chops have browned, sprinkle with crumbled sage.

• Pour wine into pan and stir to dissolve browned particles in bottom of pan. Reduce heat; cover and cook until chops are cooked through. This will depend on thickness. Medium-thick chops will cook in less than 30 minutes. Season to taste with salt and pepper. Serve with onion and sauce spooned over top.

— *Makes four servings.*

★ Parsley Potatoes

4 large potatoes, peeled, cubed
½ cup parsley, chopped
1 tablespoon butter
Salt, pepper

• Cover potatoes with water and cook until firm but tender. Drain well. Cover pan and shake potatoes gently in covered pan until surface looks slightly flaky. Add chopped parsley and butter cut into small pieces. Season to taste with salt and pepper. Shake gently again, to blend flavors. — *Makes four servings.*

TIPS/*HERBS*

• **Sage** is the seasoning most of us know from the stuffing for the Thanksgiving turkey. It has a potent flavor that must be used judiciously. Sage is also one of the easier herbs to grow and since you use so little of it in a recipe, you'll want to dry the surplus. For best results, hang plants by their stems in an airy place; a doorway is fine.

• **Italian parsley**, distinguished by flat leaves, is preferred whenever flavor is important. Curly leaf parsley is more suitable for garnishing. Cilantro, also known as Chinese parsley, is considerably more pungent in flavor and should be used only when the recipe directs.

• To keep **parsley** fresh longer, remove stems and store leaves in a covered jar in the refrigerator.

• Mince **parsley** with a sharp chef's knife or with scissors.

Liver Lover's Liver

Mushroom Salad
★ **Liver Lover's Liver**
★ **Mashed Potatoes With Skins**
★ **Pea Puree**

L iver lovers will tell you that the reason *you* don't love the stuff is that you've never tasted it cooked properly. And that means cooking it as quickly as possible.

You must start with liver that's sliced to the thinness of a blanket, say these self-proclaimed experts. Although it's possible to do this at home, it's wiser — translate that to mean infinitely easier — to ask your butcher to do the slicing for you. Since you'll want to serve the liver as quickly as possible afer cooking, you will want to fry the onions first, then at the last minute, add them to the gravy in the pan.

Pureed peas plus potatoes, cooked and mashed in their skins, make nice homey accompaniments. Add a salad of fresh, firm mushroom slices tossed with romaine, blue cheese, and an olive oil and lemon juice dressing.

★ Liver Lover's Liver

2 cups thinly sliced onions
2 tablespoons oil
¼ cup clarified butter, divided
1 pound thinly sliced calf's liver
Flour seasoned with salt, pepper
½ cup chicken stock

• Saute onions in oil until lightly browned. Set aside.

• Heat two tablespoons clarified butter in skillet. Coat liver pieces lightly in seasoned flour. Saute liver, a few pieces at a time, in hot butter. Pan should not be crowded. Liver will cook in a minute or so per side. Add more clarified butter as needed to brown all of the liver. Remove cooked pieces to warm platter while cooking remaining liver.

• When last pieces have been removed from pan, deglaze pan by adding chicken stock. Scrape browned particles from pan with a wooden spoon to dissolve them into the stock. Stir in sliced onions. Heat to a simmer. Taste and adjust seasoning. Serve onions and pan gravy over liver.

— *Makes four servings.*

★ Mashed Potatoes With Skins

3 pounds red-skin potatoes
Salt, pepper to taste
½ cup heavy cream
1 cup potato cooking water
2 tablespoons butter
1 tablespoon minced parsley

• Cook potatoes in salted water until tender (about 15 to 20 minutes). Drain well, reserving one cup of cooking water. Mash well, seasoning with salt and pepper. Add cream, cooking water and continue mashing until fluffy. Stir in butter and sprinkle parsley over potatoes.

— *Makes four servings.*

★ Pea Puree

1 package (10 ounces) frozen peas
4 large lettuce leaves
¼ cup pea cooking water
2 tablespoons butter
½ teaspoon honey
Salt, pepper

• Cook peas according to package directions, adding lettuce leaves. Reserve ¼ cup of cooking water. In blender or food processor, puree peas with reserved liquid, lettuce, butter, honey. Season to taste with salt and pepper. Heat to serving temperature.

— *Makes four servings.*

Hasty Peasant Soup

Romaine Salad
★ Hasty Peasant Soup
Crusty Bread

H asty Peasant Soup is as sturdy and practical as its name. The soup starts with lots of chopped onion and shredded cabbage sauteed in a rather modest amount of butter. Although you could use another meat (leftover turkey, maybe), ham perks up the soup's flavor nicely and you can use supermarket sandwich ham, cut into neat cubes.

Many tasters liked the big spoon of grated cheese (Parmesan or Romano) melting in each bowl at serving time. Serve the soup with crusty peasant bread and butter, and a romaine salad with anchovy garlic dressing.

★ Hasty Peasant Soup

¼ cup butter or margarine
5 cups shredded cabbage
1 large onion, chopped
1 can baby limas (1 pound), drained
1 (16-ounce) package frozen mixed broccoli,
green beans, pearl onions and red peppers
½ pound cooked ham, cubed
¼ cup uncooked rice
3 chicken bouillon cubes
6 cups boiling water
Salt, pepper
Grated Parmesan or Romano cheese

• Heat butter in large kettle. Saute cabbage and onion until vegetables begin to soften. Add drained limas, frozen vegetables, ham and rice. Cook, over medium heat, for five to 10 minutes, stirring to coat vegetables with butter and cook evenly.

• Dissolve bouillon cubes in boiling water. Add to contents of kettle. Bring to a boil, reduce heat, then cook uncovered for about 25 minutes or until flavors blend and rice is done. Season to taste with salt and pepper. If soup seems too thick, add more water. Serve hot with grated cheese.

— *Makes eight servings.*

Winter Pear and Ham Salad

Black Bean Soup With Sherry
★ **Winter Pear and Ham Salad**

Winter Pear and Ham Salad is a big salad that is sturdy enough to be served as a skier's lunch or supper. The recipe is extremely flexible. If the fruit bowl holds fresh, perfectly ripe pears, they would be our first choice for the fruit. Lacking that, we'd suggest a good quality, firm canned pear, packed in fruit juice if possible for fewer calories and less sweetness. Apples, pared or with skins on, could also be substituted.

If you need extra heft in the meal, start with a big cup of canned black bean soup spiked with sherry.

★ Winter Pear and Ham Salad

6 large pears, ripe but firm (or one
No. 2½ can of pears)
Lemon juice
4 slices (about ⅛-inch thick) boiled ham
3 ounces cream cheese, softened
½ cup good mayonnaise
2 tablespoons milk
1 teaspoon honey
2 teaspoons curry powder (more, if desired)
¼ cup pecans, walnuts or toasted almonds

● Pare pears, if desired. Core and cut into chunks. Toss gently with lemon juice. If canned pears are used, drain, cut into chunks. The canned pears need not be tossed with lemon juice.

● Slice ham into julienne strips. Blend cream cheese, mayonnaise, milk, honey and curry powder. (Omit honey if canned pears are used.) Toss gently with pears, ham and nuts.

— *Makes four servings.*

Meatless

This quick and easy burger is made from a surprising ingredient: mushrooms. Served with the usual fixings, it makes a flavorful lunch.

Ten-Minute Piecrust Pizza

Minestrone
★ Ten-Minute Piecrust Pizza

Although a full-fledged Italian vacation may be months or years away for most of us, we can have a feast of Italian flavors in just 30 minutes. Our meal begins in the easiest way possible, with a good canned minestrone made even better by embellishing each bowl with Italian parsley and lots of freshly grated Parmesan cheese.

Before serving the soup, slip a Ten-Minute Piecrust Pizza into the oven. The pizza, which takes no more than 10 minutes to assemble, uses a circle of ready-made pie pastry for the base. The pastry, a relatively new product, is sold in packages of two and is found in the same refrigerated case with ready-to-bake biscuits.

Each pastry circle makes one pizza, enough for two servings. The unused pastry in the package can be stored in the refrigerator for weeks.

We tested the pizza's vegetable topping two ways. In the first version, the vegetables were sauteed before they were put on the pastry for baking. In the second, the vegetables were placed on the pastry raw and liberally sprinkled with olive oil. We found the latter preferable.

★ Ten-Minute Piecrust Pizza

> 1 12-inch round piecrust pastry
> Cornmeal
> ⅓ cup virgin olive oil
> 1 large sweet onion, peeled
>   and thinly sliced
> 2 ounces provolone, thinly sliced
> 1 long (about 12 inches) Italian
>   or Japanese eggplant, thinly sliced
> 1 small sweet red pepper, diced
> 2 ounces Fontina, cut into small cubes
> 8 cherry tomatoes, cut in half
> Fresh parsley or oregano, chopped
> Salt and red pepper flakes to taste

• Place pastry on oiled pizza pan sprinkled with coarsely ground cornmeal. Brush pastry with small amount of the olive oil.

128

• Spread onion slices evenly over surface of pastry. Arrange slices of provolone over surface, and top with eggplant slices arranged around circumference. Sprinkle center of pastry with sweet red pepper pieces. Space Fontina evenly on eggplant slices. Cover center of pastry with tomato halves, cut side up. Sprinkle with chopped parsley or oregano.

• Pour remaining olive oil evenly over pizza. Season with salt and red pepper flakes. Bake for 10 minutes on center shelf of preheated 500-degree oven. If top needs browning, place under broiler for a minute or two.

— *Makes two servings.*

TIPS/*PIZZA*

• **Italian pizzeria pizzas** are made with bread dough of varying thickness although pizzas made in private homes in Italy often have yeast pastry foundations.

• With our current taste for **lighter foods**, modern pizzas are more likely to have thinner crusts and to contain a variety of vegetables in the topping.

• **Roman pizzas** are tomato-less and topped with onion and oil.

• **Foccacia**, the pizza of Genoa, is eaten as a bread, often with cheese.

• **Neapolitans** think that their region's classic pizza is at its best fresh from a brick oven.

Quiche McKaiser

With one bow to McDonald's and another to Quiche Lorraine, this combination includes a quiche filling of beaten egg and cream and crumbled cooked bacon baked inside a Kaiser roll. (For a meatless version, use bacon-flavored bits.) There's a bonus in the form of grated Parmesan cheese sprinkled inside the buttered, hollowed-out bottom of the roll that serves as the quiche crust and over the buttered top half of the roll that is toasted in the oven while the filling bakes.

Sound complicated? It's not, and what's more, it's as delicious as quiche and much more portable for lunch. For breakfast, try one served with freshly squeezed tangerine juice. Although tangerines tend to fall apart when you're squeezing them for juice, you can squeeze any stray segments by pressing them through a strainer with the back of a spoon.

★ Quiche McKaiser

6 Kaiser rolls
6 large eggs
¾ cup heavy cream
2 tablespoons soft butter
¼ cup grated Parmesan cheese
12 slices bacon, cooked, crumbled,
* or ⅓ cup bacon-flavored bits*

• Slice each roll horizontally using serrated knife. The top slice or lid should equal about one-third of roll. Set lids aside.

• Remove most of soft bread from bottom portion of roll to make a shell to hold filling. Do not tear crust because filling will leak out. If any bread remains in shell, press it down with spoon or with your hand.

• Beat eggs with cream or process until smooth in processor or blender. Butter inside of shell and inside surface of remaining lid half of roll.

• Sprinkle buttered surfaces with cheese, dividing cheese among the six rolls. Place half the crumbled bacon or bacon-flavored bits over cheese in shells. Place shells on baking sheet. Divide filling among the six shells; sprinkle remaining bacon over top. Bake shells and lids in preheated 350-degree oven for 15 minutes or until filling sets.

• Note: Because the bacon and cheese are salty, you probably will not want to add salt; if you do, add the salt to taste when you are mixing the eggs and cream for the filling.

— *Makes six servings.*   130

Pesto Nuovo

Antipasto
★ **Pesto Nuovo**
Pasta
Breadsticks

P esto, a summertime passion for many of us, has many virtues, including fast, easy preparation and great flavor. But a low calorie count is not normally among them. Made the traditional way with lots of Parmesan cheese, olive oil and pine nuts, the uncooked, basil-scented sauce for pasta can be a real jolt in the diet.

Enter Pesto Nuovo. Our intriguing, equally fast and easy version of the classic Italian sauce has a secret ingredient: tofu.

A meal that features the pesto-sauced pasta could begin with an antipasto of marinated artichoke hearts, black olives, cheese and roasted peppers. Crispy breadsticks would be another nice accompaniment.

★ Pesto Nuovo

1 clove garlic, peeled
½ cup fresh basil leaves
1 square fresh tofu (see note)
1 teaspoon olive oil
Salt to taste
Fresh basil leaves, for garnish

• With the food processor's motor running, drop garlic through the feed tube, and, using pulsing motion, chop it very finely. Add basil leaves and process until basil also is finely chopped.

• Cut the bean curd into large cubes, and drop through the feed tube with motor running. Add olive oil and salt, and blend until fairly smooth. Pesto should have a slightly grainy texture. Serve with well-drained, still-hot pasta. Garnish with fresh basil leaves.

• Note: Tofu will keep for about a week refrigerated in a covered container. Cover the tofu with spring water, and change the water daily for best results.

— *Makes one serving.*

Spanish Potato Omelet

```
★ Spanish Potato Omelet
★ Super Tomatoes
```

P otato omelet is one of Spain's most popular dishes, and that's under-
standable. What is surprising is that this quick-to-fix, delicious dish
hasn't become an American standby as well.
   It's easy to make. Sliced potatoes sauteed in oil make the filling. The omelet
is a matter of beaten eggs and salt.
   Eggs are wonderfully inexpensive, as are potatoes. About the only ingredient that could be considered pricey is olive oil, and that is used in modest
amounts that won't bash the budget.
   This is a slightly different omelet in that the filling is not added after the
omelet is cooked but instead is blended in with the omelet mixture and the
partially cooked omelet is flipped to brown the top.
   Don't fret about flipping. If you use a heavy pan with a nonstick surface
and have a large spatula or pancake turner, you should have no trouble
turning the rather sturdy omelet.
   To accompany the omelet, serve seasoned slices of ripe tomato. Make a lot.
They'll go quickly.

★ Spanish Potato Omelet

4 medium new potatoes, cooked, cooled
3 tablespoons olive oil, divided
6 large eggs
Salt

• Peel potatoes and slice thinly. In heavy skillet, heat two tablespoons of
the oil and cook potatoes until they begin to color and crisp. Remove from
pan and keep warm.
• In same skillet, heat remaining oil. Beat eggs and salt. Pour into hot
pan. When eggs begin to set, carefully top with potato slices. Using a
spatula, lift corners of omelet and tilt pan to allow uncooked egg to go
under cooked edges. When the omelet is cooked but still moist-looking on
top, slide it from the pan to a heavy plate. Invert the pan over the plate
then turn so plate is on top and wet side of the omelet is in contact with the
cooking surface of the pan. Cook a minute or two. Serve warm, cut in pie-
shaped wedges. Can also be served as an hors d'oeuvre, warm or cold.

— Makes four entree servings or eight hors d'oeuvres.

★ Super Tomatoes

4 large fully ripe tomatoes
Salt, pepper
6 large basil leaves, chopped
1 teaspoon fresh lime juice
½ teaspoon sugar
1 clove garlic, minced
1 tablespoon olive oil

• Peel tomatoes by immersing in hot water just until peels begin to split. Place in cold water immediately to cool. Skins will pull off easily.

• Slice tomatoes into half-inch thick slices. Season lightly with salt and freshly ground pepper, basil leaves, lime juice, sugar and garlic mixed with olive oil. Allow to stand, covered, at least 15 minutes before serving.

— *Makes six servings.*

Our Favorite Eggplant

Boston Lettuce Salad
★ Avgolemono Soup
★ Our Favorite Eggplant
Couscous

Our Favorite Eggplant is an unusual recipe in that it doesn't require deep-frying to be flavorful. Brush the eggplant slices on both sides with a little garlic-flavored oil and broil five minutes to a side. When you've done this, sprinkle lightly with low-fat mozzarella and put under the broiler again. To serve, just heat some homemade or store-bought spaghetti sauce (or a can of good-quality stewed tomatoes), and place the eggplant slices over top. Sprinkle well with chopped parsley and some crumbled goat cheese (chevre or feta will do nicely).

Complete your fast and easy low-calorie meal by starting with a cup of Greek Avgolemono Soup, a soup that looks rich and creamy but is actually a calorie-watcher's dream. Add instant couscous to sop up the surplus sauce, and serve a salad of Boston lettuce for balance.

★ Our Favorite Eggplant

3 small eggplants
2 tablespoons garlic oil (see note)
Salt, pepper
¼ pound low-fat mozzarella, shredded
2 cups spaghetti sauce
   or 1 can (14½ ounces) stewed tomatoes
3 tablespoons chopped parsley
¼ cup crumbled goat cheese

• Wash eggplants, but do not peel them. Remove stems. Slice vertically into quarter-inch-thick slices. Brush each slice on both sides with garlic oil. Place a single layer of eggplant slices on a nonstick cookie sheet. Broil five minutes per side, seasoning with salt and pepper as you turn slices.

• Sprinkle with mozzarella and return to broiler for a minute or two or until cheese melts.

• Heat sauce and spoon onto a platter. Arrange overlapping slices of eggplant over sauce. Sprinkle parsley and cheese down the center of the eggplant slices.

• Note: Garlic oil can be made by placing two bruised cloves of garlic in one-quarter cup of olive oil and allowing to stand overnight. Use leftover oil for cooking or salads.

— *Makes four servings.*

★ Avgolemono Soup

4 eggs
Juice of 2 lemons
4 cups chicken broth
Salt and pepper to taste

• In a large bowl, beat the eggs, gradually adding lemon juice. Heat the broth in a large saucepan. Slowly add broth to eggs, beating vigorously. Return soup to heat, and stir just until thickened. Season to taste. Do not allow soup to boil. Soup may also be served cold.

— *Makes four servings.*

TIPS/*LEMONS AND MORE*

• When you use **lemons** for juice, don't waste the flavorful rind. Grated lemon rind mixed with granulated sugar makes a lovely offbeat sweetener for breakfast grapefruit, fruit salad or hot oatmeal mixed with raisins. The grated rind alone can add a nice flourish to a simple green salad. Toss warm, butter-sauteed walnuts with grated lemon rind for another good salad topping.

• **Avgolemono Soup** lends itself to a number of variations. To make the hot soup heartier, add cooked rice; to make it hot and elegant, use cooked white and wild rice. Cold soup looks prettier and is richer if you top each bowl with a dollop of sour cream, a teaspoon of salmon caviar and a sprig of fresh dill or mint.

• For a **fish version** of avgolemono, strain a quart of good homemade fish stock and use it to replace the chicken stock in the original recipe.

Minestrone Salad

Chilled Tomato Soup
★ Minestrone Salad
★ Basil-Parmesan Dressing
Hot Garlic Bread

You've probably tasted gazpacho, the Spanish soup that's the equivalent of a liquid salad. Now try Minestrone Salad, a big, hearty summer salad that's inspired by the soup of the same name. The combination of colors and flavors is impressive, and chopping and a small amount of cooking are the only real work involved. Minestrone Salad would make a superb summer lunch or supper prefaced by a chilled tomato soup and served with hot garlic bread.

★ Minestrone Salad

¼ cup chopped scallions
½ cup sliced carrots
½ cup chopped celery
1 cup cooked rice
1 cup diced zucchini
1 cup canned garbanzos, drained
½ cup cooked green beans,
    cut in 1-inch lengths
2 cups shredded cabbage
1 cup cherry tomatoes, halved
1 cup cooked elbow macaroni
1 cup Basil Parmesan Dressing (see recipe)
Salt and pepper to taste
Spinach leaves
Fresh basil leaves
Grated Parmesan cheese

• Toss scallions, carrots, celery, rice, zucchini, garbanzos, green beans, cabbage, cherry tomatoes and elbow macaroni with Basil Parmesan Dressing. Let stand several hours to blend flavors. At serving time, taste again, adjust seasonings and add salt and pepper to taste. Serve on a platter lined with fresh spinach leaves. Garnish with basil leaves, and sprinkle with freshly grated Parmesan cheese.

— *Makes six to eight servings.*

★ Basil-Parmesan Dressing

¾ cup olive oil
¼ cup red wine vinegar
1 clove garlic, minced
¼ cup fresh basil leaves, finely chopped
Freshly ground pepper

• Place ingredients in a jar with a tight-fitting lid, and shake well to blend. Use as directed in Minestrone Salad recipe.

— *Makes about one cup.*

Spicy Szechwan Bean Curd

> **Cucumber Salad**
> ★ **Spicy Szechwan Bean Curd**
> **Noodles With Toasted Walnuts**
> **Stir-fry Cherry Tomatoes**

Bean curd will seem bland beyond belief if you taste the pillowy squares of soy protein before they are combined with other, more assertively flavored ingredients. But add a spicy sauce and you'll understand why so many Asian cuisines feature dishes with bean curd.

Spicy Szechwan Bean Curd is a good example. Here, slices of bean curd are lightly marinated in a soy and wine mixture, then stir-fried with ginger and garlic and wood ear mushrooms. The marinated bean-curd slices get a final jolt of seasoning with the last-minute addition of a hot and sour sauce. In a Chinese meal, you would serve this with several other dishes. For a Western meal, cherry tomatoes stir-fried with garlic, buttered noodles with toasted walnuts and cucumber salad would be satisfying.

★ Spicy Szechwan Bean Curd

3 wood ear fungus
¼ cup soy sauce, divided
2 teaspoons cornstarch, divided
2 teaspoons sherry
1 pound fresh bean curd
2 cloves garlic
2 thin slices ginger
3 tablespoons vegetable oil
1 tablespoon hot bean paste or chili sauce
½ teaspoon sugar
1 tablespoon rice vinegar
½ teaspoon sesame oil
1 tablespoon chicken stock

• Soak wood ears in enough warm water to cover for a few minutes. Make a marinade by combining three tablespoons of the soy sauce, one teaspoon of the cornstarch, and the sherry. Cut bean-curd squares in half, then cut each half into slices about three-quarters of an inch thick. Toss bean curd gently with the marinade.

• Chop garlic finely. Shred ginger slices. Drain and coarsely chop the wood ears.

• Heat vegetable oil in large wok or skillet. Saute garlic and ginger over high heat for 10 seconds. Remove bean curd from marinade with slotted spoon. Add to garlic mixture and stir-fry for two minutes. Add wood ears and continue cooking for one minute.

• Add marinade to the mixture in the wok. Blend hot bean paste with remaining soy sauce, the sugar, vinegar and sesame oil. Stir into mixture in wok. Blend remaining cornstarch with chicken stock. Stir into mixture in wok. Cook, stirring, until sauce thickens. Serve over buttered noodles with toasted walnuts.

— *Makes two servings.*

TIPS/*BEAN CURD AND MORE*

• **Bean curd** is an important ingredient in the home cooking of Szechwan, where the white bland-flavored cakes are made in a process similar to that used for cheese.

• Chinese Buddhists have religious objections to killing animals for food and use bean curd to make **a dazzling array** of foods textured to resemble meat, poultry or fish.

• **Wood ear fungus** goes by a variety of names. The edible fungus, which is widely used in the cooking of Szechwan is also called cloud ear, tree ear or Judas' ear. A dried wood ear is dime-size, slightly wrinkled and dark gray or brown in color. Soaking in boiling water takes about 15 minutes and brings out the oddly gelatinous texture. It's a good idea to pick over the soaked wood ears to remove embedded debris.

Gingered Tofu and Peppers

Marinated Green Beans or Asparagus
★ Gingered Tofu and Peppers
Brown Rice

Tofu is a veritable sponge when it comes to absorbing other flavors. A two-inch square has no cholesterol, practically no saturated fat and 9.4 grams of protein. Fresh tofu comes in a variety of textures. Japanese-style is usually sold in water and is very soft, delicate and fragile. Chinese-style tofu has some of the water pressed out. It's firmer. Pressed tofu is sold dry and can be cooked in vigorous stir-fry dishes.

For our quick-cooking Gingered Tofu and Peppers, we'd recommend the slightly firmer Chinese-style tofu, which will hold its shape through the browning process.

Bottled oyster sauce, used in the recipe, is available wherever Asian cooking supplies are sold. Experience has taught us to ask the grocer to recommend a good-quality sauce. The more expensive brands generally have richer, truer flavor. Tofu is also sold in Asian food stores and an increasing number of supermarkets.

The finished dish is substantial enough to serve, with brown rice, as a dinner entree. We'd like it preceded by marinated green beans or asparagus.

★ Gingered Tofu and Peppers

4 sweet red peppers
2 tablespoons vegetable oil
1 tablespoon finely chopped fresh ginger
4 squares tofu
1 to 2 teaspoons bottled oyster sauce

• Wash peppers. Remove seeds. Cut peppers into 1-inch squares. Heat vegetable oil in large skillet or wok. Add peppers and saute briefly until they begin to soften. Add ginger to skillet. Cut each tofu cake into nine cubes. Add tofu cubes to skillet, stirring and sauteing until tofu cubes are lightly browned on all sides. Add bottled oyster sauce. Taste and add more oyster sauce if desired.

— *Makes four servings.*

Mushroom Burgers

Lentil Soup
★ Mushroom Burgers

M ake burgers with a new and easy recipe that substitutes mushrooms for meat and gives flavorful results. Serve the burgers in the traditional way, on a round roll with a thick slice of sweet onion, vine-ripe tomato, favorite condiments and potato chips and you'll find that they'll please all but the most die-hard meat-eaters.

To make a heartier meal, preface the burgers with lentil soup that you have made from scratch or bought canned. Spike the soup with some sherry and hot pepper sauce to taste and sprinkle with a handful of finely chopped sweet red pepper for color. You could also substitute French fries (made from frozen French fries) for the potato chips.

★ Mushroom Burgers

1 pound mushrooms, sliced
1 large onion, minced
¼ cup oil, divided
2 slices firm white bread, finely diced
2 tablespoons Chinese oyster sauce
    (see note)
1 egg, lightly beaten
Salt and freshly ground pepper to taste

• In a large skillet, saute sliced mushrooms and minced onion in two tablespoons of the oil for about four minutes. Stir in bread and oyster sauce, and cook for one more minute, stirring frequently. Remove mushroom mixture from pan, and cool. Stir in beaten egg.

• Wipe pan clean, and heat. Add remaining oil and spoon mushroom mixture into hot oil in six equal amounts. Spooned mixture will hold together with cooking. Brown on one side, then turn with a large spatula and brown the second side. Season with salt and pepper. (Oyster sauce is salty, so additional salt may not be required.)

• Note: Chinese oyster sauce can be purchased in Asian groceries or the specialty sections of some supermarkets.

— *Makes six servings.*

Green Tomato Welsh Rabbit

★ **Mustard Slaw**
★ **Green Tomato Welsh Rabbit**
 Corn Muffins

If you beat the frost to your tomato plants, there's the question of what to do with all the green tomatoes you have harvested. They're dandy for mincemeat, for pies and conserves. But the easiest, most immediate use for the tomatoes that have arrived too late to ripen in the sun is to make fried tomato slices.

Scan any vintage American cookbook and you'll probably find at least one recipe for this early autumn specialty. Some like them sweetly fried, sprinkled with brown sugar and served with a creamy gravy. Then there are those who prefer a cornmeal crust and no sauce. Still others prefer the simplicity of a simple seasoned-flour dusting before frying.

The last method is one that makes the perfect fried tomato for our Green Tomato Welsh Rabbit. Here fried slices are served with a quick and easy cheese sauce and a topping of crisp bacon or bacon-flavored bits. Traditional Welsh rabbit is served on toast but here the tomato slices substitute for the bread. For a brunch or supper menu, you might add bought or mix-made corn muffins and a crunchy cabbage slaw dressed with Dijon mustard vinaigrette.

★ Green Tomato Welsh Rabbit

---

1 teaspoon dry mustard
1 teaspoon Worcestershire sauce
¾ cup beer
4 cups shredded medium-sharp
  Cheddar cheese
Hot pepper sauce to taste
2 eggs, lightly beaten
4 large green tomatoes, cut in
  ½-inch slices
Flour seasoned with salt and pepper
¼ cup cooking oil
8 crisp-cooked bacon slices
  or ¼ cup bacon-flavored bits

• In the top of a double boiler over simmering water, heat the dry mustard dissolved in Worcestershire sauce and beer. When mixture is warm, begin stirring in cheese, about a cup at a time. Add hot pepper sauce to taste. (A drop or two should be sufficient.) When all the cheese has been incorporated, remove one-half cup of melted cheese from the double boiler, and stir into lightly beaten eggs. Return this egg and cheese mixture to the contents of the double boiler. Cook for about three minutes or until mixture is thickened.

• While sauce is cooking, dip tomato slices in seasoned flour. Heat oil until it begins to sizzle. Fry tomatoes until nicely browned on both sides. If necessary, reduce heat to keep flour coating from overbrowning. Serve immediately. For each serving, cover three or four tomato slices with one-quarter of the cheese sauce, and top with two crisp bacon slices or a sprinkling of bacon-flavored bits.

— *Makes four servings.*

★ Mustard Slaw

2 cups cabbage, chopped for slaw
3 tablespoons olive oil
1 tablespoon wine vinegar
1 teaspoon Dijon mustard
Salt, pepper to taste

• Toss cabbage with other ingredients, which have been well-blended. Flavor improves with standing.

— *Makes four servings.*

143

Zucchini Pancakes

Tomato Slices
★ Zucchini Pancakes
★ Creamed Mushrooms

Zucchini Pancakes treat your family to a fast, nutritious meal. Similar to potato pancakes, these main-dish patties can be made with carrots, potatoes and any other vegetable firm enough to grate. Serve them for lunch or dinner with curry mayonnaise or sour cream and salmon caviar or topped with Creamed Mushrooms. For breakfast or brunch, they would be delicious with chive-sprinkled scrambled eggs and bacon or sausage links. In any case, some big ripe tomato slices would make a colorful salad addition.

Make the pancakes half-size and they're a unique appetizer.

★ Zucchini Pancakes

> 2 cups grated zucchini
> Salt
> ⅓ cup grated Parmesan cheese
> ⅓ cup all-purpose flour
> ½ teaspoon baking powder
> 4 eggs
> 2 tablespoons minced green onions with tops
> 2 teaspoons lemon juice
> Mayonnaise or sour cream
> Dill weed for garnish

• Place the grated zucchini in a colander. Sprinkle with salt and let stand for 10 minutes.

• In medium bowl, stir together grated cheese, flour, baking powder. Beat in eggs, onions and lemon juice until thoroughly blended. Press excess moisture from zucchini and stir zucchini into egg mixture.

• For each pancake, drop one-third cup batter onto hot well-greased griddle or skillet (380 degrees for electric griddle). Cook until golden brown on both sides. Serve hot.

• For appetizer-size cakes, use two tablespoons batter each. Serve with mayonnaise or dairy sour cream garnished with fresh dill weed, if desired.

• **Carrot variation:** Substitute shredded carrot for zucchini.

• **Potato variation:** Substitute shredded potato for zucchini and add one-

144

quarter teaspoon salt to dry ingredients.

— *Makes six pancakes (two entree servings) or 16 appetizer servings.*

★ Creamed Mushrooms

½ pound mushrooms, sliced
1 small onion, chopped
2 tablespoons butter
1 tablespoon flour
1 teaspoon chicken bouillon granules
½ cup boiling water
½ cup heavy cream
Salt, pepper to taste

• Saute mushrooms and onion in melted butter for about five minutes or until mushrooms have released much of their liquid. Stir in flour and chicken bouillon granules and add boiling water. Cook, stirring, until sauce is thickened. Stir in heavy cream and heat to serving temperature. Do not boil or cream will curdle. Season to taste.

— *Makes two servings.*

TIPS/*HERBS AND MORE*

• **Fresh herbs** add interesting flavor to vegetable pancakes. Add snips of lemon thyme or basil to zucchini; chervil or mint to carrots; chive or sage to potatoes.

• **Creamed mixtures** like the mushroom recipe here change character with herbal additions. Add chopped fresh dill and the mushrooms will taste like something from Old Russia. Stir in some pesto and the mushrooms go Italian.

• To make **fresh pesto**, blend two cups fresh basil leaves (stems removed) with one cup Italian parsley (stems removed), one cup grated Romano cheese, one cup extra-virgin olive oil, two peeled garlic cloves and a handful of ground pine nuts. Use over hot drained pasta or as directed in tip above.

The Philadelphia Inquirer / BONNIE WELLER

Warm Coffee Zabaglione brings a meal to an elegant close. No one needs to know that you whipped it up in under 10 minutes.

There was a time when I made and served elaborate desserts because it seemed expected of someone whose livelihood is writing about food.

Eventually I realized that my health-conscious family and friends were eating the desserts I served but, afterward, feeling guilty about all those calories, all that butter and sugar.

Moreover, those fancy cakes and croquembouche required more time and effort in the kitchen than I — and most of the cooks I knew — had to spend. I abandoned them in favor of the simpler yet no less stylish sweets that follow.

I've never regretted it.

Warm Endings

★ Crunchy Baked Nectarines

3 small fresh nectarines
⅓ cup butter or margarine
⅓ cup brown sugar, packed
3 tablespoons flour
1 cup walnuts, chopped
Ice cream

• Halve nectarines; discard pits. Place nectarines, cut sides up, in nine-inch pie plate. Combine butter, sugar, flour and walnuts in small saucepan. Bring to a boil over medium-high heat, stirring often. Mound nut mixture on nectarine halves. Bake in a 350-degree oven for 25 minutes or until tender. Serve with ice cream.

— *Makes six servings.*

★ Apricots Flambe

16 fresh apricots, halved, pits removed
3 tablespoons butter
3 tablespoons brown sugar
(or more if necessary)
¼ cup dark rum
1 pint vanilla ice cream

• Saute apricots in butter until slightly softened. Add sugar to pan and stir to blend with butter. Heat rum and ignite with a long match. When flame dies out, serve warm apricots over ice cream.

— *Makes four servings.*

★ Strawberry-Buttered Omelet

3 large eggs
3½ tablespoons sugar, divided
1 tablespoon rum
Pinch salt
2 tablespoons Strawberry Butter
  (see recipe)
2 tablespoons sour cream
2 large fresh strawberries for garnish
2 sprigs mint for garnish

• Separate eggs. Beat yolks until frothy with one tablespoon of the sugar and the rum. Add the salt to the egg whites and beat until soft peaks form. Add remaining sugar and beat until stiff but not dry. Fold whites into yolks. Pour mixture into heated well-buttered omelet pan or skillet. Place pan on middle rack in oven. Bake at 325 degrees for 20 minutes.

• Remove omelet from oven, place Strawberry Butter on one side and fold the other side over. Turn onto warm plate and serve at once with sour cream. Garnish with a strawberry and a mint sprig.

— *Makes two servings.*

★ Strawberry Butter

¼ pound (1 stick) unsalted butter
½ cup strawberry jam
1 teaspoon lemon juice

• Soften butter. Whip and blend in jam and lemon juice. Place in covered container and refrigerate until ready to use. Butter may be frozen and used later for a delicious spread on toast, waffles or quick breads.

— *Makes about ¾ cup.*

★ Rum-Sauteed Banana Slices

4 small firm-ripe bananas
1 tablespoon butter
1 teaspoon brown sugar
2 tablespoons rum

• Slice bananas thickly. Melt butter in small skillet and add banana slices. Saute five minutes; sprinkle with sugar and continue cooking, stirring constantly, for five minutes. Pour rum over mixture in pan and flame, stirring constantly. Serve warm over rum-raisin ice cream or with whipped cream.

— *Makes four servings.*

★ Bananas Brulee

8 large bananas, peeled
¼ cup coffee-flavored liqueur
1 cup heavy cream
2 egg yolks
½ cup confectioners' sugar
½ teaspoon vanilla

• Slice bananas in half vertically. Place the bananas in a shallow baking dish large enough to hold the pieces side by side. Add the liqueur. Place in a preheated 400-degree oven until bananas are heated through, about three minutes.

• Meanwhile, beat cream until soft peaks form. Stir in egg yolks, confectioners' sugar and vanilla. Beat until firm peaks form. Spoon cream mixture evenly over bananas. Return to oven, and heat for three more minutes. Remove from oven.

• Heat broiler. Place banana and cream mixture under the broiler, and brown the surface. Watch carefully; topping burns easily. Serve immediately, spooning liqueur over each serving.

— *Makes eight servings.*

★ Nutty Baked Apples

6 large baking apples
Pecan halves
Cinnamon
Honey
1 cup water

• Wash apples. Core and place in baking dish. Fill centers with nuts and sprinkle with cinnamon. Spoon honey to fill the well in each apple. Add water around apples in baking dish. Place filled apples in microwave baking dish, cover with plastic wrap and cook at high for 20 minutes.

• To bake in conventional oven: Cut apples into small pieces and mix with remaining ingredients. Cover with foil and bake at 375 for about 20 minutes or until tender.

— *Makes six servings.*

★ Banana Trifle Cake
With Hot Fudge Sauce

1 small frozen poundcake
(about 14 ounces)
2 tablespoons dark rum or sherry
1 cup cold milk
1 package (3½ ounces) vanilla instant
pudding and pie filling
1 cup sour cream
2 large firm, ripe bananas
Hot Fudge Sauce (optional, see recipe)

• While cake is still frozen, slice it horizontally into two layers of equal thickness. Defrost cake and sprinkle both cut sides with rum or sherry.

• Mix milk with pudding mix, and beat at low speed until well-blended, a minute or two. Blend in sour cream. Let pudding set for five minutes, in the refrigerator, to firm before using to fill cake.

• Place one cake layer, cut side up, on serving plate. Top with half the pudding mix. Slice one banana, and arrange slices in filling.

• Top with second cake slice, cut side down. Spread remaining filling over top of cake, and decorate by slicing remaining banana and arranging attractively over top of cake. Serve immediately. If desired, spoon Hot Fudge Sauce over each serving.

— *Makes four to six servings.*

★ Hot Fudge Sauce

½ cup unsweetened cocoa powder
¾ cup sugar
⅔ cup evaporated milk
⅓ cup light corn syrup
5 tablespoons plus 1 teaspoon butter
1 teaspoon vanilla

• Combine cocoa and sugar in saucepan. Blend in evaporated milk and corn syrup. Cook over medium heat, stirring constantly, until mixture boils. Boil and stir for one minute. Remove from heat. Stir in butter and vanilla. Serve warm. Leftover syrup can be refrigerated and reheated in saucepan over low heat.

— *Makes two cups.*

★ Coffee Zabaglione

4 egg yolks
1 teaspoon sugar
¼ cup coffee-flavored liqueur

● Using whisk or hand-held beater, beat egg yolks with sugar until thick and lemon-colored. Stir in liqueur. In top of double boiler over hot water, cook egg mixture, whisking constantly, until thick as heavy cream. Do not allow to boil, or eggs will curdle. Pour into tall, stemmed glasses, and serve warm. (May also be chilled to serve later).

— Makes two servings.

Sauces and Toppings

★ Peanut-Crunch Topping

½ cup crunchy-style peanut butter
¼ cup melted butter
¼ cup sugar
1½ cups coarsely crushed oatmeal cookies

● Combine peanut butter, butter and sugar; toss with oatmeal cookies. Serve over fresh pear wedges.

— Makes enough for four to six servings.

★ Hard Sauce

½ cup butter (1 stick) softened
1 cup confectioners' sugar
1 egg white
Brandy or rum, to taste

● Cream butter with sugar. Beat in egg white and brandy or rum. Refrigerate. Serve over warmed poundcake or fruitcake slices.

— Makes about 1½ cups.

★ Almond Yogurt Topping

1 package (3 ounces) cream cheese,
  softened
1 cup almond-flavored yogurt (see note)

● With electric mixer, beat cream cheese until fluffy. Fold in yogurt. Serve over berries or fruit.

● Note: If almond yogurt is unavailable, substitute vanilla yogurt to which you add a few drops almond extract, or use plain yogurt, sugared to taste and flavored with almond extract. If desired, garnish with slivered, toasted almonds.

— *Makes six servings.*

★ Lemon Cream Topping

1 container (8 ounces) soft cream cheese
¼ cup sifted confectioners' sugar
2 tablespoons milk
1 tablespoon lemon juice
1 teaspoon grated lemon rind

● Combine ingredients, mixing until well-blended. Serve over slices of good-quality poundcake.

— *Makes 1⅓ cups.*

★ Easy Chocolate-Bar Fondue

½ pound milk-chocolate bar
⅓ cup light cream
1 pound grapes, washed, dried

● Break chocolate bar into pieces. Melt chocolate in fondue pot or on top of double boiler. Add cream. Stir to blend. Serve warm with grapes.

— *Makes six servings.*

★ Warm Apricot-Rum Sauce

½ cup apricot preserves
1 tablespoon dark rum

● Heat preserves until they begin to melt. Stir in rum and blend well.

Serve immediately over good-quality vanilla ice cream.
— *Makes enough for four servings.*

★ Raisin-Butter Frosting

¼ cup dark or golden raisins
¼ cup butter margarine, softened
½ teaspoon grated lemon rind
1 tablespoon lemon juice
¼ cup milk
3½ cups sifted confectioners' sugar

• Chop raisins finely. Beat all remaining ingredients together until light and fluffy, then blend in raisins. Use to frost plain cake.
— *Makes enough to frost one cake.*

Make-Ahead Desserts

★ Kiwi Fruit Fool

6 large kiwi fruit
Sugar
1 pint heavy cream

• Remove skins from fruit. Mash with sugar to taste. Whip cream. Fold sweetened, mashed fruit into cream. Serve in tall glasses. If desired, garnish with a slice of kiwi fruit.
— *Makes four servings.*

★ Peaches in Red Wine

6 ripe peaches
1 lemon, cut into six pieces
Vanilla sugar (see note)
1 bottle red wine

• Peel the peaches and slice them into large goblets. Squeeze one piece of lemon over each peach, and sprinkle with vanilla sugar. Cover peaches with red wine and let them sit a few minutes to improve flavor.

• Note: To make vanilla sugar, split a vanilla bean lengthwise and bury it for a few days or weeks in granulated sugar in a covered jar. Replace the sugar as it is used; one vanilla bean will flavor sugar for months.
— *Makes six servings.*

★ Strawberries Royale

1 pint strawberries
⅓ cup orange liqueur
½ cup heavy cream
2 tablespoons sugar

• Marinate whole strawberries in orange liqueur for 15 minutes. Puree half the berries. Whip heavy cream with sugar. Fold in puree. Spoon over whole berries.
— *Makes two to three servings.*

★ Almond-Plum Dessert

1 pound Italian prune plums
1 lime
½ cup sugar (or more, to taste)
1 cup almond yogurt (see note)
Chopped toasted almonds (optional)

• Wash plums and remove pits. Grate lime rind over plums. Squeeze juice from limes and add to plums with sugar. Taste and adjust sweetness. Stir well. Cover with plastic wrap until serving time. Serve with almond yogurt, passed separately or layered, parfait-fashion, and a garnish of chopped toasted almonds.
• Note: If almond yogurt is unavailable, use vanilla yogurt seasoned with a few drops almond extract.
— *Makes six servings.*

★ Cantaloupe-Ginger Sorbet

2½ cups cantaloupe puree
½ cup Ginger Syrup (see note)
¼ cup lime juice

• To make cantaloupe puree, remove rind and seeds from cantaloupe. Cut into large chunks and blend until smooth in a blender or food processor.

Mix puree, Ginger Syrup and lime juice. Pour into container of a frozen-dessertmaker, and freeze according to manufacturer's directions.

● Note: To make Ginger Syrup, combine ½ cup sugar, ½ cup water and 1 tablespoon shredded fresh ginger in a microwave-safe bowl. Heat at full power until sugar dissolves, about two minutes. Cool and strain out ginger. Syrup may also be cooked in a small pan: Heat to boiling, then reduce heat and stir until sugar dissolves.

— *Makes four servings.*

★ Ricotta Custard

1 cup ricotta cheese
Chocolate bits
Chopped toasted almonds
2 teaspoons heavy cream

● In the jar of a blender or the work bowl of a food processor, process ricotta cheese until smooth. Remove from container and add a handful of chocolate bits, some chopped toasted almonds and heavy cream. Chill until serving time.

— *Makes four servings.*

★ Brownie Pie

½ cup butter
3 (1 ounce) squares
*   unsweetened chocolate*
1¼ cups sugar
¼ cup flour
Pinch salt
¼ teaspoon vanilla
3 large eggs
¼ cup chopped pecans

● Melt butter and chocolate in double boiler. Beat in sugar. Fold in flour and salt. Add vanilla. Beat eggs, fold into chocolate mixture with nuts. Turn into a greased 9-inch pie pan. Bake at 350 degrees for 20 to 30 minutes. Center should be moist. Do not overcook. Serve warm with ice cream.

— *Makes six servings.*

★ Nougatina

¼ cup sugar

1 egg yolk

2 tablespoons orange liqueur
*   or orange juice*

1 teaspoon grated orange rind

1 carton (15 ounces) ricotta cheese

1 cup dried fruit and nut mix

• Stir sugar, egg yolk, orange liqueur or juice and orange rind with cheese to blend well. Stir in fruit and nut mix. Chill.

— *Makes six servings.*

Index

159